Edwin Abbott Abbott

Cambridge sermons, preached before the University

Edwin Abbott Abbott

Cambridge sermons, preached before the University

ISBN/EAN: 9783337085933

Printed in Europe, USA, Canada, Australia, Japan

Cover: Foto ©ninafisch / pixelio.de

More available books at **www.hansebooks.com**

CAMBRIDGE SERMONS

PREACHED BEFORE THE UNIVERSITY.

BY THE

REV. EDWIN A. ABBOTT, D.D.

FORMERLY FELLOW OF ST. JOHN'S COLLEGE, CAMBRIDGE.

London:
MACMILLAN AND CO.
1875.

LONDON:
R. CLAY, SONS, AND TAYLOR, PRINTERS,
BREAD STREET HILL.

TO THE

REV. J. LLEWELYN DAVIES, M.A.
Rector of Christ Church, Marylebone

This Volume

IS GRATEFULLY DEDICATED

BY ONE WHO HAS FOR TWENTY YEARS

DERIVED FROM HIS TEACHING

GUIDANCE DURING YOUTH AND STIMULUS DURING MANHOOD

HEARING FROM HIS LIPS

THE GOOD NEWS OF CHRIST

Digitized by the Internet Archive
in 2008 with funding from
Microsoft Corporation

http://www.archive.org/details/cambridgesermons00abbouoft

PREFACE.

OF the following Sermons, those on Faith and Science formed a course intended to be preached before the University of Cambridge in the February of this year. Owing to illness, the third was not preached.

The two on Prayer and Work were preached at Cambridge in the year 1870.

I have taken the opportunity of this publication to add a sermon preached at Westminster Abbey in 1869. I was importuned at the time to publish this sermon, in order to vindicate myself against an accusation brought against it, that "it was of a nature to set class against class." But, as the Sermon was preached without the aid of the manuscript, and probably varied considerably from the manuscript in its oral form, it seemed clear that for the purpose of vindication such a publication would have been, at all events at the time, quite nugatory: and there were other circumstances not now worth detailing, that rendered the publication just then impossible.

But now, on re-reading the manuscript, it appeared to me that, at this interval of time, I might be able to convince the few who might be interested in being convinced, that, at least in its general tenor, the sermon was not of a nature to "set class against class:" moreover, some parts of the sermon seemed to me to commend a tendency to Reform, which, however on the increase, still requires much inculcation before it is likely to attain its due force. For these reasons I have ventured to publish the manuscript, although it covers, to some extent, the same ground as is covered by the Sermon on Work, preached at Cambridge in the following year. I must add that the Westminster Abbey Sermon was written to be spoken, not to be read; though revised, it contains several abrupt expressions and rhetorical terms scarcely adapted for reading. But however it may be æsthetically faulty, it contains nothing of which I am morally ashamed.

If indeed a preacher may be fairly accused of "setting class against class" because he cannot help betraying a feeling of profound dissatisfaction with the present state of religious feeling and religious action, then I must plead guilty to the charge. For, optimists though we may be in our hopes as to Christ's future Kingdom on earth, yet surely we are allowed, nay, bound, to feel profoundly dissatisfied with our present miserable realization of it. We look around and see Christ supplanted, abroad by a Church, at home by a scheme of salvation or a sacramental dogma: many among the educated classes of our countrymen throwing away the name of Christians without having ever really apprehended what is meant by faith in Christ; and—perhaps the most pitiful spectacle of all—in a large number of fairly intelligent believers, we see a tremulous Christianity, looking despairingly to the future, and paralysed for all the noble aggressive purposes of a Christian Church by a vague horror of the future, by a terrible dread that the belief in a God may be exploded next year, through the unearthing of some new fossil demonstrative of the Darwinian theory, or that the Divinity of Christ may be subverted by the discovery of a couple of Uncial Manuscripts: and, as a consequence of this superstition and this faithlessness, we see the Church, which once led the world, now lagging behind and even retarding it in the path of progress. Seeing all this, who may not be excused for feeling somewhat dissatisfied with our present form of Christianity? Some one said in Roman times that it was inconceivable that two Augurs could meet without laughing: at the first glance it might seem no less true that two Christian ministers ought hardly to be able to meet without sorrow too deep for tears.

Yet such an epigram is scarcely justified by a comparison of this century with the past. If there is more conscientious disbelief now, there is also less unconscientious conformity. If, for example, at the Universities young men are less willing than they once were to take holy orders, yet at least they no longer take orders so readily as they once did to gain a fellowship or to fill a living. It is a striking evidence of the freer play of conscience in these times that at the present moment two or three valuable fellowships in one small college at Cambridge are not, and cannot be, filled, owing to the restrictions that limit them to clergymen. Such rewards, often conveying a small competency for life without the necessity of the slightest effort, are very tempting to young graduates without independent means and uncertain as to the choice of a profession: all the more creditable that the bribe is so generally resisted. If Mephistopheles wished to sap the foundations of the English Church, he could not do better than assume the shape of some Master of a College influential enough to bolster up for another quarter of a century these obsolete and pernicious clerical restrictions. As believers in Christianity we may regret that men are less ready than they once were to identify themselves with our form of the Christian religion: but, as believers in Christ, we must rejoice to see the rising generation acting with a sincerity and an honesty that betoken the true influence of Christ's own Spirit.

It is not altogether surprising that young men are unwilling — perhaps unduly unwilling — to enter the ranks of the clergy. Modern criticism, not to speak of science, has so altered, or seems so likely to alter, the aspect of many passages in the Bible, that a man scarcely knows what is meant, or to what he is committing himself, by accepting the Scriptures as the Word of God. The old belief in the scientific accuracy of the Scriptural account of the Creation of the World is now generally rejected; the belief in the literal interpretation of the metaphorical expressions relative to the future state of souls after death, is also rapidly disappearing; it is beginning to be acknowledged even by orthodox and popular writers that some parts of the miraculous narratives in the Old and New Testaments may be based upon the misunderstanding of poetical or metaphorical expressions; and thus the truth is dawning upon most educated Christians in the Church of England that they must no longer hope to dispense with the use of thought, judgment, and conscience, by leaning upon the infallibility of a book any more than by leaning upon the infallibility of a Church. Consequently, some of the laity—little guessing how far their difficulties, and often many more serious difficulties are shared by the clergy, and unaccustomed to distinguish faith in Christ from assent to the historical accuracy of the details of scriptural narrative — scarcely venture to call themselves Christians, though they are, in reality, some of Christ's sincerest followers: and others of the laity, having been taught from childhood to treat the Bible as an inseparable whole, as soon as they find doubt thrown upon a single verse or word of it, throw off at once their faith in the Bible, and in Christ and in God.

Yet we ought not to despair. We are in a time of transition and expectation waiting for fresh light: and light will come, nay, is coming, from science, from criticism leavened by science, from the history of the past, from the social experiences of the present. All these influences will combine to cast new light on the life and work and character of Christ. No doubt we may have to give up something. Truth is often inclosed and preserved for centuries in a hard shell of error; in time the shell is burst and cast away. So may it be perhaps with Christianity. Much that we have been accustomed to think kernel, may prove to have been a mere shell and temporary covering. Yet, in return for such losses, great may be our gain if it should be revealed that faith and trust in Christ are of a simpler nature than was once supposed, following naturally from faith and trust in goodness.

Meantime it is our wisdom to wait, and, as long as we are in the twilight, not to move on rapidly, as though we were in the full brightness of noon. If we will but be ready to make all truth welcome, light will come to us in God's good time. There is even now at least light enough to show us certain works to which Christians cannot be wrong in devoting themselves during this age of waiting; and indeed the very act of faithful waiting has been consecrated for ever as a divine work by our great poet:—

They also serve who only stand and wait.

Besides, it will be a gain that, so far as we can wait in patience and silence without doing violence to our conscience, we should do nothing to produce a discontinuity in the National Religion. The best way, perhaps the only right way, to uproot error, is to plant truth. Unless we are sure about our planting, the uprooting is a doubtful benefit, often rooting up truth with error. As it has been for the most part in our English State, so let us hope it may be in our English Church, that we may, if possible, follow the traditions of our nation in avoiding all revolutions, all dislocating shocks, all sudden subversions and uprootings: rather let us hope for a gradual and continuous development of religious knowledge eliminating error mainly by the appropriation and assimilation of fresh truth, and thus, step by step, leading us through Christ nearer to the God of our fathers, to Him to whom on the strength of our past National history, we may hopefully appeal for the future of our nation: *O God, we have heard with our ears, and our fathers have declared unto us, the noble works that thou didst in their days and in the old time before them.*

CONTENTS.

	PAGE
PREFACE	vii

FAITH AND SCIENCE—

    I.—INTRODUCTION   1

    II.—THE CREATION OF THE WORLD   23

    III.—THE CREATION OF MAN . .   48

CHRISTIAN WORK   73

CHRISTIAN PRAYER . .   95

THE SIGNS OF THE CHURCH .   121

SERMONS.

FAITH AND SCIENCE.[1]

I.—INTRODUCTION.

I will praise thee, for I am fearfully and wonderfully made; marvellous are thy works, and that my soul knoweth right well.—PSALM cxxxix. 14.

IF Anaxagoras, exiled for his heresy on the nature of the sun, had been supernaturally enabled to look forward to the rise of a new religion introduced by Him who called Himself the Truth, he might have sighed that he had not lived in those happier and less superstitious times, when no honest seeker after truth could possibly be persecuted by those who called themselves Truth's servants. If his gaze into the future had been so far extended that he could see a Christian astronomer recanting, under the coercion of Christian priests, a truth soon afterwards denied by none but lunatics,

---

[1] Of the three sermons on Faith and Science, the first deals with their relations generally, the second is devoted to the creation of animate and inanimate nature, and the third to the creation of mankind.

he might have declared in haste that all religions are the same—equally dishonest, or equally blind. But if yet two more centuries of the future had been added to his vision, so that he might have seen the grand truths of geology discovered, and no sooner suggested than opposed, or at least suspected, by the large majority of pious Christians, then indeed he would have said that the religion of Christ was inferior in its love of truth to the religion of his idolatrous countrymen: for they at least sinned once or twice only, whereas with the disciples of the Truth, opposition to the Truth seemed to have become an inveterate habit. Lastly, had he looked onward, yet a few years further, to the questions that are now occupying the world touching the development of life and the origin of man, discerning the same spirit of distrustful antagonism or alarm, might he not have exclaimed of Christian views about science, as some one is said to have exclaimed of history, *Do not tell me what the disciples of Truth say about science; for what they say must be false*"?

No doubt we have extenuating circumstances to allege. Scientific men may sometimes have been prone to mix their theological inferences with their scientific facts, as though the two were inseparable: "If my thesis is true, there is no God; or, which is much the same, we cannot know whether a God exists; or, supposing Him to exist, we know not what is His nature." Taking them at their word the Christian, who has made up his mind that there is a God, has not thought it worth while to discuss the scientific thesis. Again, men of science may have sometimes appeared to be unfair, because they have taken little account of important aspects of humanity comparatively familiar to other people. Devoting themselves almost exclusively to the absorbing pursuits of science, and leaving themselves scarcely leisure enough to consider with sufficient care the emotional side of human nature, they may have fallen into the habit of thinking, upon too slight grounds, that there are no things in heaven and earth but what can be analysed in their laboratories. And this bias, this erroneous but honest prejudice, assuming the appearance of unfairness, may have disgusted and deterred some from so much as considering the theories of science.

But surely disgust and anger are out of place here. Surely this one-sided, unevenly developed nature, this unscientific habit of scientific dogmatism outside the province of science—supposing it to exist—is its own sufficient punishment. If a man be what is called an "infidel," does he not demand our compassion? But if, moreover, he is an honest and industrious infidel; if—not to supplant a rival in science, not for love of money, not for love of fame, but mainly for the love of truth—he devotes days and nights to the persevering, wise, and successful investigation of nature, then must we not say that such a man, "infidel" though he may be, is, in a certain sense, the servant of the Eternal Truth, shewing forth God's glory, not with his lips but in his life? And for us, Christians, is not our duty clear? Are all God's warnings in the history of Christendom to go for nothing with us? Having erred twice at least and having been convicted of error, shall we a third time err? In the face of past experience ought we not to give up our suspicious dread of that part of God's revelation which is called Science, and instead of shrinking, instead of timidly acquiescing, instead of coldly accepting, ought not we, the children of light, thankfully and reverently to welcome fresh light, from what source soever it may come?

"But what if modern discoveries appear to contradict the language of the Scriptures? Must we not fear that our faith will be shaken?" I propose to touch on this objection in a future discourse; meantime I will content myself with asking, Has our faith, I do not indeed say in the letter of the Scriptures, but in Christ, been shaken by the admission that the sun does not move and therefore could not be arrested in its course by any human voice, or by the admission that death was in the world even before man was created and therefore before man could possibly have sinned? If our faith has not been shaken, if rather it has been confirmed and widened and purified by discoveries, at first seemingly subversive of faith, then surely there is some ground for the presumption that as a result of the discoveries made in the present and to be made in future generations, we shall grow into a deeper reverence, a nobler faith, a more implicit trust in God our Maker, in proportion as we attain to a knowledge that this mysterious universe, and we the human tenants of this one planetary speck of it, have been far more *fearfully and wonderfully made* than had been dreamt of in our theology.

In any case we must fall back upon this truth, which ought to be a truism—that we have no more right to shut our eyes to the teaching of the world than to the teaching of the Bible, that if He inspired the authors of the Scriptures, He also created the world. By the word of the Lord were the heavens made: yes, and the earth and the sea also, with all their generations of inhabitants, vegetable and animal, engaged in perpetual conflict with each other, conquering, spreading, developing, then in turn succumbing, dwindling, perishing—all this is, in some sense, the Lord's work. The Psalmist was not afraid of this terrible enigma, the tree of life rooted in the corruption of death; he seems to have felt that God might take a pleasure in it: *Thou hidest thy face, they are troubled: thou takest away their breath, they die, and return to their dust. Thou sendest forth thy spirit, they are created: and thou renewest the face of the earth;* and, a moment afterwards, *The glory of the Lord shall endure for ever: the Lord shall rejoice in his works.* Nor is it alone

God the All-wise and Unsearchable that can contemplate with pleasure this mysterious scene of blended creation and destruction; even His frail human servant, the faithful singer of Israel, can cry: *I will sing unto the Lord as long as I live: I will sing praise unto God while I have my being. My meditation of Him shall be sweet: I will be glad in the Lord.*

Let us Christians, with surely far more cause for sweet meditations and songs of praise, endeavour to imitate the faith and trust of one who lived under what we are in the habit of calling "an inferior dispensation." Let us be sure that nine-and-twenty centuries ought not to have passed, cannot have passed, without revealing to us much in natural philosophy, much also in the history of man, which must convey to us some new revelation of the Divine nature. And in the same confident spirit of gratitude with which we regard the past discoveries of science, let us also entertain the present, and anticipate the future. I do not indeed maintain that the existence of a Creator, still less that His nature and attributes, can be absolutely demonstrated by arguments derived from the phenomena of the Universe. Pain and death perhaps, sin certainly, must always remain an unsolved riddle for us. If we could believe that the Supreme Good is not omnipotent, a solution would be possible; or, if we could believe that the Omnipotent is not supremely good, that also would be a solution; or, if we could believe that sin is not evil and not against God's will, a third solution would be open to us. But as we can believe none of these things, as we must hold fast to the faith that God is supremely good and also supremely powerful, and that He hates sin, and yet that sin is in the world, we are shewn at once by our own confession to be illogical, exiling ourselves altogether from the sphere of logical demonstration.

Exiles from rigid logic we must be content to be, whenever we mortals speak of the nature of God; but that is no cause why we should dispense with reason altogether. Life and the affairs of life do not altogether depend upon demonstration; but they are not uninfluenced by it. We act for the most part not upon absolute demonstration, but upon a mixed proof, part of which appeals to our reason, while part appeals to our faculties of faith and hope. The same kind of proof may naturally influence our religious belief. The impossibility of ever reconciling, in accordance with the rigid rules of logic, the existence of a supremely good, all-powerful, eternal being with the existence, even for a moment, of any shape of evil, must be apparent to any thoughtful child, much more to men. Still, various appeals may be made even to the reason, in favour of our belief. For example it ought to have some weight, at least for those who have not altogether rejected the possibility of the existence of a God, to point out that our belief, illogical though it may be, is morally strengthening. It is a dangerous doctrine, no doubt, to teach that one may believe whatever is useful to believe; yet to some extent, carefully watched and restricted, it is a reasonable inference for those who believe in a Supreme Good, that whatever belief about God produces moral good in man must have some elements of truth.

Again, although, logically, even the momentary existence of a speck of evil is incompatible with the existence of the God adored by Christians, yet in practice we are so constituted that our belief in Him becomes easier in proportion to the probability that Evil subserves Good, or that Evil is gradually being conquered by Good; and this probability—though finding its firmest basis in history and the ordinary experience of our daily lives—may, as I think, be strengthened by reference to the discoveries of science relating to the pre-historic periods.

If, for example, it is suggested that, from the creation of the world till now, there has been a continuous progress in the beauty and order of created things, if science herself should prove that conflict and death have been made subservient to this progress, eliminating the less fit and leaving the fittest to survive; if it should appear that even the fall of mankind was in some sense a rise, that sin was the necessary consequence, in our imperfect nature, resulting from the dawning revelation of a perfect external will; if it should be suggested that all the struggles and agonies of animate creation, and all the sins of men did in some sense eliminate imperfection and evil and prepare the way for successively higher degrees of good; or, to use the technical term of science, if it should appear that a Natural Selection based upon force prepared the way for a Natural Selection based upon cunning or skill, and that skill in turn gave place to order and discipline and social union, and, lastly, that narrow selfish social ties gave way to a Natural or Divine Selection (or shall we say a Divine Inclusion?) based upon the all-embracing and all-conquering love which was first introduced into the world, not as a philosophic precept but as a spiritual power, by Jesus of Nazareth—then, while contemplating the æonian process of conforming humanity to the divine image, shall we not naturally feel that our faith is confirmed instead of being shaken? Shall we not be grateful to science for proving, or even suggesting, that we have more cause than ever for saying with the Psalmist: *I will praise thee, for I am fearfully and wonderfully made: marvellous are thy works, and that my soul knoweth right well?*

Yet never let us forget that our religion must always be a faith, a hope, not a demonstrated certainty. Whatever light Science may shed upon God's works, never dream that she will ever demonstrate His attributes by her analysis. Science can but shew us link after link in the chain of cause and effect, revealing links by myriads where we had recognized them by tens, proving complexity, proving beauty, proving order, but not proving God; no, in the name of Faith and Hope, no. For, if such proof were possible, what would be the result? Suppose, for a moment, that the highest attributes of God could be demonstrated in the same way in which we can demonstrate a proposition of Euclid — could be discerned as clearly as we discern that two and two make four. What then? *The things that a man seeth*, says St. Paul, *why doth he yet hope for?* and we may add, *the things that a man absolutely demonstrates, how can he yet have hope or faith about them?*

No: let Science demonstrate our God, and Hope and Faith are banished for ever. What then becomes of St. John's *victory that overcometh the world, even our faith?* Where would be the victory of Faith, when the battle had been already gained by Reason? Such a state may be reserved for us hereafter in a higher condition of existence, when Faith and Hope may be needless, finding their fulfilment in sight; but that state is as yet far off. Even the love of children for their earthly parents is based in part upon faith and trust, and seems sometimes to be contradicted instead of being supported by facts. How much more natural is it that this should be true of our love for the invisible Father whom no man hath seen nor can see!

Christianity therefore is a faith, a hope. Let

our enemies even say, if they will, that it is a self-enforcement to believe what we wish to believe: there is some truth in this, and it is not a truth of which we need be ashamed. Faith *is* a self-enforcement, a perpetual struggle against what we believe to be our lower self, against a spirit of hopelessness, against a spirit of suspicion, against a spirit of impurity, and above all against that most fatal spirit of cynicism which always puts the worst construction on human actions, which resolutely refuses to admire or to love, which sneers at enthusiasm, which, like the slanderer in "Othello" "is nothing if not critical," and which is the best possible representative of that mysterious Evil whose slanderous influence we call diabolic.

In this battle of faith, the world—I mean this visible material world—may be our ally or our enemy. If we could see in it nothing but capricious beauty, fantastic semblance of order, confusion everywhere and everywhere struggle, without a sign to show whither victory is inclining—then the world becomes our foe. We might still trust in God, but we should trust Him in spite of His handiwork, not in any way because of it. The Psalmist rapturously asserts that *the heavens declare the glory of God, and the firmament sheweth His handiwork:* but we should cling to God in spite of the heavens and maintain our faith in Him in defiance of His firmament.

This would be a most melancholy, a truly deplorable condition, surely not to be acquiesced in without an effort. Yet I am persuaded that we are in danger of falling into a state of this kind by reason of our unwillingness to face and discuss the discoveries of science. The enemies of Christianity tell us that science is to crush the religion of Christ. In a few cynical remarks, contained in a recent review on the late Canon Kingsley, you may have read lately that "for people who want a cheerful bracing creed it is a good thing to be optimists," but it is added that events "have made it increasingly difficult to follow the wholesome propensity of men to find an opinion true as soon as it is found to be edifying." Now, as I read science, events are making it, if anything, easier and not more difficult to follow this wholesome propensity. Never has the Person of Christ towered in sublimer majesty above the bickerings of theologians and sceptics, revered and loved by the combatants of either side; never have scholarship and history seemed so likely to combine to help us to a higher comprehension of Christ's character, and a purer, simpler trust in Him and in His Holy Spirit; and never before has science shed such a lustre on the wonders of God's works, revealing progress where we had fancied relapse, and law where we had been able to see nothing but caprice. Certainly, if it was true in St. Paul's time, it is far truer now that *the invisible things of Him from the creation of the world are clearly seen, being understood by the things that are made, even His eternal power and Godhead.*

We are warned emphatically by a foremost apostle of Science, that we are to beware of the sin of rejecting her gospel; a minister of God has no other choice but to endorse that warning, and to bid you, the disciples of the Truth, accept truth thankfully from every source. We will do more than this: we will not only listen to the authoritative inculcations of science, we will even lean forward to catch her whispers, her conjectures, her floating fancies. For the term "discoveries of science," like many other terms in common use, is used in very different senses. Sometimes it is used, with strict propriety, of the proved and established facts of science; but at other times it is used to include almost certain, or very probable, or barely probable, hypotheses; lastly, it sometimes includes the mere guesses or conjectures of science, some of which draw, very largely indeed, on what has been called the scientific imagination. But, for our purpose, facts, hypotheses, conjectures, imaginations, let us, on the present occasion, for argument's sake, suppose them all to be true, at least so far as regards their general tendency; and let us ask ourselves whether their tendency is not of a nature to shew us that we are, in the words of the Psalmist, to an extent hitherto undreamed of, *fearfully and wonderfully made.*

One only discovery or conjecture of science I would desire to omit from consideration. It is the theory that man is an automaton; that what we call volition has no more to do with causing or controlling our actions than the rising blood in our cheeks has to do with causing our sense of shame or indignation. "Just as the blush is no more than the bodily expression, so our will is no more than another kind of expression—call it mental if you will—of a certain condition of the brain. Our bodily actions proceed from physical changes in our brain, just as the motion of a bell results from the touch upon the handle; as for our will, it is but a signal of what has been going on in the brain, just as the bell's sound tells you that the bell has been moved. To say that the will causes the action is as absurd as to say that the bell's sound causes the bell's motion."

I omit consideration of this subtle speculation because it can hardly, by any possibility—though it may seem a paradox to say so—ever become practically interesting. Now and then a poor wretch, hurrying down the road to ruin, may smooth and precipitate his descent by working himself into the belief that he is an irresponsible machine; but with the mass of mankind it will always be inherent, automatically if you like, to regard both themselves and others as *not* being automata. Indeed, it has been well remarked that, according to this theory, even the man of science—or shall we say the scientific automaton—can hardly, upon his own theory, blame the automatic theologian for obeying the impressions of brain, in rejecting automatism. But I have thought it not unsuitable to mention this interesting speculation or discovery, because it would appear to shew that Science, no less than Theology, has its points of collision with common sense.

But to return to our subject. The common characteristic of "the discoveries of science" taken in the wide sense indicated above, appears to be the demonstration that the world is not so simple in its structure as it was once supposed to be. Ancient theories, like ancient maps, of the world, often interest us by the childlike faith with which a rude symmetry, an obvious, regular simplicity, are taken for granted. It is often assumed for instance, that water, or fire, or some other known element, must have been the origin of all things, that the country inhabited by the theorist must be the exact centre of the earth, the earth being surrounded by a circular ocean, and our world, of course, being the centre of the solar system.

As men have been anthropomorphic in their notions of God, so have they been in their theories about the formation of God's world. They have assumed that God must have created the universe in all respects as they would have created it, had they been in His place, that is, not only in the shape that was most familiar to them, but also in the way that seemed to them most striking and significant of power. Consequently men have supposed that the world must have been made in a moment, and at a word; or at least, that each several part of the world must have been thus made. Preparation, growth, development—to ascribe these quiet processes of familiar nature to the hand of a creating God, seemed perhaps to early theorists a derogation from His Majesty, and incompatible with the Omnipotence of the Creator. Doubtless even now we are still retarded in our understanding of God's universe by imputing our thoughts to Him; but at least we have learned to believe that the world is far more complex than it was once supposed to be. Age after age has opened up the view of further and still further causes indefinitely multiplying the links in the chain of creation, and strengthening the belief that the world as well as man is *wonderfully made*.

Fearfully and wonderfully made, says the Psalmist; and he gives thanks to God for it. *I will praise thee, for I am fearfully and wonderfully made; marvellous are thy works, and that my soul knoweth right well.* The thought of growth and development, of imperfect humanity gradually fashioned is not abhorrent to him: *Thine eyes did see my substance yet being imperfect: my substance was not hid from Thee, when I was made in secret and curiously wrought in the lowest parts of the earth.* Surely this is the right feeling with which we should welcome each revelation of the complex nature of God's handiwork.

Take a lesson from any flower, from a common daisy—which to a very young child appears almost a sentient thing, almost a person with a character of its own, a being incapable of division into distinct parts, or, to an older child, divisible indeed, but divisible in some obvious arbitrary way, into a yellow ball encircled with a fringe of white. Now comes the botanist with his analysis, and straightway the yellow ball, placed beneath the microscope, reveals itself as a disk within a circle or ray, both ray and disk composed of a host of individual florets, each with functions for the reproduction of the flower; and the white fringe resolves itself into a host of separate leaves, each with a shape and beauty of its own, once the protection and now the ornament of the composite interior; and the green stem is revealed, not as a mere pillar and support, but as the conducting-pipe of nutriment, and then the roots as subterranean feeders—and thus, each part in turn and each part of a part being divided and subdivided, the child's daisy, the Person with a Fairy character, or the yellow circle in the ring of white, vanishes for ever to give place to the man's daisy *fearfully and wonderfully made.*

That daisy is our world. To us also, with our childish fancies about the earth on which we tread and the beings that are its tenants and the heavenly bodies that give us light, comes science and takes heaven and earth to pieces before our eyes, lengthening our gaze upward to new planets, new suns, new systems, while beneath our feet she throws open to us undreamed of secrets down to the very centre of our planet, and there, where we had seen nothing but so much clay or stone fresh as it came from the Creator's hand, she exhibits to us layers of deposited life, generations after generations of living beings that have passed away, everywhere complexity within complexity, everywhere growth, everywhere development, æonian growth, æonian development.

Why should not this new revelation of the wonders of the universe fill us with the same wholesome pleasure and admiration blended with reverence which is inspired by the contemplation of the structure of a little flower? Perhaps the reason may be that to some of us the purpose apparent in the daisy is not so clearly revealed in the structure of the world. It is, of course, not so easy to discern the purpose of a vast and complicated plan as of a small portion of the plan. We are soldiers fighting in the battle-field of good against evil; now it is a well-known military proverb that scarcely the general himself, much less the private soldier, can comprehend the movements of a battle as a whole. The purpose and object of this or that regiment's charge, the reason for the assault on a particular battery, or the unflinching costly defence of a particular piece of ground, details like these may be partially intelligible to the private soldier, but even these not always; and as for the larger and grander movements of a battle or a campaign, why one division retreats while another moves forward, why one town is protected and another sacrificed, for these and similar movements he cannot pretend even to offer a conjecture. Now if the Christian theory be admitted, that Good has been from a time inconceivably distant, waging war against Evil, the purpose that we shall hope to see manifested in the creation of the world will be the destruction of Evil. Unmixed good we shall not hope, as yet, to see; that would be the same thing as hoping that the battle could be gained before it had been begun. Evil perpetually manifested and in many cases subordinated to good: ugliness, monstrosity, conflict, pain, death, ferocity, ignorance, selfishness, sin in its thousand subtler shapes—all this we shall be prepared to see, but we shall hope to see it mitigated, destroyed, yes, more than destroyed, converted in each case into some germ of goodness. If we can see this darkly, this is all that we can now expect to see: and, seeing it, we shall discern a purpose in the battle of creation. Darkly, very darkly—be prepared for this—will the purpose of God in His works be discerned even by His most faithful children. But if science helps us to discern it less darkly than before, then we must bless science not only as science, but also for suggesting that there is a Supreme Good by suggesting that all things evil have a tendency to good.

But perhaps it may be felt by some of you that gradual progress is not so clear a testimony to God's presence as a number of special creative acts. Yet does this feeling, on serious reflection, seem to spring from a worthy conception of God? That God should be for the most part as it were absent from His universe, but that on a few special occasions when a crisis arises, when some old phase of creation is to pass away, and a new one is to succeed, He should step in to impart a special impulse to His flagging instrument—this may be so; though, if it is so, it will possibly be found hereafter that these, which we call special acts, are really in accordance with some divine vast order, occurring just as a comet might recur in a period of a thousand or a million years. But will it be less worthy of Him, will it not rather be worthier, if science should prove that there were no such special sudden creative acts, that God was always present everywhere directing and shaping all things by the slow and quiet processes of pre-ordained laws?

Suppose two celestial artists at work in rivalry to create some machine of beauty, some instrument that shall call up before the eye innumerable pictures, all different, all pleasurable, and all original—the imitation of nature being excluded as one of the conditions of the contest. The first, with infinite labour, by innumerable special acts, creates innumerable patterns, which he exhibits one by one, each a perfection of beauty: but the second, by the force of his celestial will, enacts the simple laws of light, and then calls forth a million pictures, each different, each pleasurable, and each original, out of a simple tube in which a dozen beads are shaken at random between two little mirrors—out of a child's kaleidoscope. Which of these two creators is the more divine?

Now, in the shifting pictures of our terrestrial kaleidoscope if we could discern nothing but good and evil, ugliness and beauty, irregularly and inextricably confused, then we might perhaps suppose that the universe came together by chance, or that the complicated machine had fallen into some disorder passing the artist's wit to remedy. Or again, beneath many apparent imperfections had we discerned some latent law, but still no law of progress, then we might recognise an imperfectly good or imperfectly powerful artist, who could excite in us no higher feeling than amazed bewilderment. But, if science points not only to a law, but also to a law of progress; if science reveals to us a few simple elements, like so many mere splinters of glass, restrained within the barriers of two or three natural restrictions (the laws of motion, suppose), and out of these jostling fragments if we see some kind of law emerging, not kaleidoscopic but progressive—call it, if you like, a divine selection or natural selection, or a struggle for existence—in which, as I have hinted above, each lower quality, after triumphing over a lower than itself, is developed to its highest, and then makes way for a higher than itself, so that force, skill, and social instinct, in turn, give place each to the next best, preparing the way for the best of all, for Love, the future Lord of the world—if this is what Science thinks she can reveal, or reveals without thinking what it is she is revealing, surely from the contemplation of a series of pictures such as these, studied under the strong light shed by Him who is the Light of the world, the Christian may arise, as much an optimist as the old Hebrew Psalmist: *I will praise thee, for I am fearfully and wonderfully made; marvellous are thy works, and that my soul knoweth right well.*

FAITH AND SCIENCE.

II.—THE CREATION OF THE WORLD.

I will praise thee, for I am fearfully and wonderfully made; marvellous are thy works, and that my soul knoweth right well.—PSALM cxxxix. 14.

CARRYING out the purpose mentioned last Sunday, let us to-day consider, rather more in detail, "the discoveries of Science" in their general tendency and their relation to our Christian faith. If you remember the plan then suggested, we are to speak tentatively, accepting, at least so far as regards their general tendency, even the suggestions and conjectures, as well as the authoritative inculcations of Science. Speaking in this tentative way let us substitute the name of God in many places where scientific men would perhaps prefer to speak of Nature, and let us ask ourselves, in each scientific assumption, is there anything that makes the Divine Name jar with the context?

I propose in this discourse to touch on the creation of the world and of vegetable and animal life, reserving for next Sunday the consideration of the creation of man. In attempting to represent fairly and, at the same time, briefly, certain statements of science, it may be found impossible to avoid the mention here and there of scientific details and terms, some of which may seem too technical for the pulpit. For this I would apologise if I did not think that, to all here present, these details are likely to be intelligible, and that it is the duty of the preacher, no less than of other speakers, to speak in such a way as shall enable him to make himself most readily intelligible to his audience.

To deal first, then, with the discoveries or conjectures of astronomy. These need not occupy us long: for although they have undoubtedly and, as I think, beneficially changed the point of view from which we regard some passages of Holy Scripture, yet, partly perhaps by reason of our longer familiarity with them, partly because the nature of astronomy admits of more patent demonstration than geology or biology, the Christian mind is now ready to discuss almost any astronomical theory without grave disquietude.

Such disquietude as astronomy may suggest has assuredly not sprung from recent discoveries. As soon as any approximation was made to the real size of the heavenly bodies, there must have arisen the question that still arises within our hearts, and which we might almost express in the words of the murmuring apostles, *Why was this waste of substance made? For it might have been spent* in myriads of habitable worlds and given to mankind. Undoubtedly it would be a trying and a painful effort to suppose that stars, whose light, travelling through space towards us for thousands of years, has but just reached our planet, were created solely to give light to the inhabitants of earth. If we were bound by our religion to suppose that all the heavenly bodies that are were created solely and simply for earth's benefit, great would be the strain upon our faith.

But our religion dictates no such scientific dogmas. On the contrary, while suggesting to us that there are other intelligent creatures of God besides ourselves, it gives us scarcely a hint of the processes by which these beings may have been created; and, as for ourselves, though occasionally mentioning, in language general and metaphorical, states of æonian life and æonian chastisement awaiting us after death, the Holy Scriptures give us no detailed information as to either condition. So far as the Scriptures are concerned, every star and planet in turn, yes, even every nebulous and rudimentary beginning of a planet, may be or may have been the home of some order of God's creatures, higher or lower than our own. Some of these may be preparing their children for a life on earth, while others may be tenanted by natures once human, now being prepared for higher states of that superhuman existence upon which they have already entered.

Assume for a moment that it may be true—

though in its totality it has been scarcely put forth at present as more than a hypothesis—but assume that this earth of ours, the stores of heat being spent at last, will, after some thousands or millions of years, become an uninhabitable globe. Assume also the birth and growth of our globe in the manner conjectured and described by astronomy: first, a mere shapeless portion of a nebulous mass revolving round a centre common to the whole; then a portion appropriating shape and unity, and a motion of its own, and, in accordance with the laws of motion, taking the place assigned to it in the solar system; then, from a gaseous mass becoming a fluid mass and gradually putting forth an outer and more solid crust, but shrouded still, as are some planets even now, in a dense steaming atmosphere, rendering life impossible for natures such as ours—pointed at, perhaps, by the human inhabitants of some other world as a planet on which no human life could ever exist, a perplexing problem of waste—next, as its heat departed, and the increasing coolness made life possible, receiving —Science itself can do no more as yet than guess how—some vital germ. If, in the end, after ages of preparation for the reception of this vital germ, after ages more of development, during which life has been shaped by the Creator in a continuous progress from the first vital thing, called by whatever name, up to that higher developed ideal of mankind which, centuries hence, is to appear made like in all respects to God the

Maker, through conformity to the Son of God—if, at last, when the earth has done its work as a school of life, the worn-out carcase of our planet, emptied of its vital heat, is to be left, even like our present moon, to be a minister of light to some other planet, or to be a home for some strange kind of life to us unknown—what is there in all this at which the Christian, of all men, need feel alarm? He who can unflinchingly see committed to corruption the body of a man, God's noblest structure known to us, made in His image, can he not bear to think that there may come a time when the body of this planet may in like manner be bereft of the life that tenants it, and be mingled with other silent stars, those sons of God that cease their shouts of living praise for a season?

And if there should be any truth in the conjecture, the most strange and romantic recently put forth in the name of science, that in due course the sun is to take up the song of the starry children of God, and to become a home of life, and that, after passing through innumerable phases of development, the sun itself, the centre of our solar system, is to transfer its matter and life to some other unknown centre, some sun of suns about which our sun is conjectured to be slowly revolving—if there is any truth in this, the strangest, the wildest dream of Science, surely, so far from being a terror, it is fraught with hope, suggesting as remedies for sin and wretchedness here, other hopes in other worlds hereafter, and an ultimate though inconceivable absorption of every material object into some immaterial existence about the throne of God.

"But men are dazzled" you say, "by the mere attempt to contemplate such a vista of glorious transformations: fear of the Creator falls upon us and casts out perfect love." Fear ought not to fall upon us, at least not servile fear: only a wholesome awe not incompatible with love. Are we not rather too much disposed to an undue and slavish admiration of whatever in nature seems to us grandiose and vast? Yet in comparison with the revelation that *God is Love*, how ineffectual and pale appear even the brighest fancies of the scientific imagination? Why ought it greatly to concern us that God has moved, in accordance with certain laws, a few more millions of tons of matter for a few more millions of years than we had supposed? No doubt such knowledge is not to be despised: it is natural and right to wonder at power and order. Increased awe of order and power may produce increased reverence, and increased reverence for God may, according to the laws of our human nature, produce a corresponding increase of love; therefore Science is to be accepted as God's minister, teaching us the rudimentary lessons that God is Law and Order. But order and law are not God's most dazzling attributes. Time and space, and motion and matter, immeasurable periods and orbits, immeasurable velocities and masses, what is there in all these so very awe-inspiring and bewildering compared with the making of a man?

One of our modern poets tells us that the whole of the Andes cannot be compared for worth with the tiniest speck of animate creation. And to us Christians, of how much more value than a million of tenantless planets ought to appear a single one of those creatures, whose shape and nature and sympathies have been adopted by the Son of God! Let those to whom man is but a *quintessence of dust*, decry, if they will, our self-conceit and arrogance, and amuse themselves, with Celsus, in comparing the human race to "a group of frogs round a pool, concluding that God must be in their image, and debating who is the greatest sinner among them:" or let them say with the melancholy Pliny that "man is the most miserable of creatures inasmuch as he alone has been doomed to objectless aspirations, and desires that surpass fulfilment, while, in compensation for these evils, he has received nothing but the privilege of depriving himself of his own wretched life." Not for ourselves, but by our reverence for the Creator, are we bound to believe that He is not in the whirlwind, nor in the fire, but in the still small voice, whose quiet whispers breathing on the troubled sea of evil are subduing all things to the dominion of love. To those therefore that direct us upward, on our search for signs of the divine working, to *this most excellent canopy, the air, this brave o'erhanging firmament, this majestical roof fretted with golden fire,* we shall reply, continuing the quotation from our great dramatist: Yes, but—*What a piece of work is a man! How noble in reason! how infinite in faculty! in form and moving, how express and admirable! in action, how like an angel! in apprehension, how like a god!*

But, to return, and to sum up our remarks upon the teaching of astronomy: we contend that there are no difficulties in recent astronomical speculations beyond such difficulties, such apparent waste and such delay, as meet us on earth, in the habitual contemplation of the ordinary works of nature. It is not even proved that there is waste at all in the disposal of the heavenly bodies; and, were there ever so much apparently proved waste, it would not proportionately be greater than the waste of life that is found here daily, in every square foot of earth, and in every drop of water. Again, if there is delay in heaven, so is there delay on earth, in each of the familiar quiet processes of Nature, whenever busy in her noblest works, in the growth of the oak, in the rearing of a man, or in the formation of those great empires in which, as Bacon tells us, " men sow greatness to their posterity and succession." Our conclusion is that, while astronomy presents no contradictions to our faith that are not already known to us, it has not only for centuries past suggested to us in the most vivid manner, that God is a God of law and of order, but also, in these last days, exhibits that law of heavenly creation, as a law of development and progress, thereby stimulating us to a higher-reaching faith and ampler hopes.

And now our planet is to be supposed fitted to become the home of life: and life appears. Whence it appears Science herself can at present do no more than conjecture; nor is it the origin, so much as the history of life, that has interest for us. If indeed there were proved to be truth in the conjecture put forth, some few years ago, by an eminent man of science, that our satellite the moon may have transmitted to us not only her borrowed light, but also the germs of life, such a truth would curiously harmonize with these fancies of astronomy above mentioned; and whether it be called a theory or a conjecture or a fancy, the bare suggestion that from the midst of those volcanic craters on whose familiar specks we gaze by night, there came to us the seeds of all earthly life, the thought that we may in time transmit to other heavenly bodies what we have thus received, and that planet can thus hand on life to planet throughout the solar system, all this cannot but have a certain fascination in the mere scope of its suggestiveness.

But we should be wrong in attaching much importance to the origin of life, except so far as it illustrates some law. If planetary transmission of vital germs could be proved to be a law, that would, no doubt, be a grand law. But regarded as an isolated case of transmission, merely putting back the cause of earthly life one link further in the chain of cause and effect, this conjecture, even if established as a truth, would be of no great interest.

Indeed, are we not in danger of exaggerating the theological interest attaching to the at present unknown process by which God created the first germ of life? As a chemical question it may be of the highest interest, but need it be so very interesting theologically?

"The banishment of life"—that I believe was the motto adopted by a celebrated chemist, who devoted himself to the production of a living germ out of lifeless matter.

"The banishment of life" — a strange term surely, to denote, what ought rather to be called "the production of life!" Does one banish electricity by producing it? And, when produced, is not electricity just as much electricity, whether produced by what we call Nature, or by man, being in either case produced by God's laws? But perhaps the chemist meant to indicate that he hoped to bridge the gulf between the living and the lifeless; so as to render the distinction between the two, and therefore the name of life, hereafter unnecessary. In that case "banishing life" might be better called "banishing lifelessness;" for the object attained would amount to a proof that all apparently lifeless matter was potentially vital, just as glass may be potentially electrical. I could stand by the side of such an investigator, with good will and gratitude, wishing him God's speed on his laborious path, in the full conviction that, if he were successful, he would succeed, not by banishing God's laws, but by obeying them, and that the result of his success would probably be to elicit some new cause for *rejoicing in the name of the Lord*. Great ought to be our compassion for the weak brother whose faith in God would be shaken because a chemist should succeed next year in producing vital cells out of a hermetically sealed vessel containing only the elements of protoplasm.

Passing, therefore, over the origin, we come to the development of life. Now here, detail is impossible. To start from the more rudimentary animal organisms, such as are described as consisting of "an assemblage of cells arranged on little branching stems and tufts .... often erroneously spoken of as sea-weeds,"[1] in which the animal element is exhibited as emancipating itself, so to speak, from the "inert membrane"[2] by which the contractile substance in all plants is limited and fettered, and as thereby passing from vegetable into animal life; and from this, or from some such origin, to attempt to trace the development of life up to and beyond the leviathans whose skeletons are the wonder of our museums, this would obviously

[1] Jukes, "Manual of Geology," p. 213, Edinburgh, 1873.
[2] Cohn, quoted by Professor Huxley, "Critiques and Addresses," p. 88.

be, on the present occasion, impossible. But the origin of all these vital forms, and the law or laws suggested by science as the shaping causes of this varied, yet on the whole continuous, development, may be far more briefly stated, and deserve our careful consideration.

It is suggested then—not proved, but suggested as increasingly probable—that from some finite number of original germs of the lowest type of life all higher forms of life have been derived, without subsequent special creative acts,—without any interpolations, so to speak, of supplementary creation. Our leading physiologist, expressing himself with all the more weight because he is revising and modifying a previous expression of opposite opinion, says: "When we turn to the higher vertebrata, the results of recent investigations, however we may sift and criticize them, seem to me to leave a clear balance in favour of the evolution of living forms one from another"— an evolution which he elsewhere speaks of as "progressive modification." Connected with, but of course not depending upon, the theory of evolution, is the supposition that, on the whole, there has been a tendency to introduce complexity of organization, or, to quote the words of Sir Charles Lyell,[1] "that the invertebrate animals flourished before the vertebrate, and that in the latter class fish, reptiles, birds, and mammalia made their appearance in a chronological order, analogous to

[1] Lyell's "Principles of Geology," vol. i. p. 164.

that in which they would be arranged zoologically, according to an advancing scale of perfection in their organization."

Assuming the fact of evolution, we are next led to ask—"What is the evolving principle?" and the answer contains one of the greatest mysteries of nature. There are other subordinate principles, as will be shortly seen: but the fundamental principle at work in the development of life is death—lavish, illimitable death. The instinct of each race prompts it to increase beyond the bounds of the sustenance provided for it by nature: as it increases, the competition among individuals of the race for the necessary share of food becomes keener; the stronger individuals of the race, a small minority, obtain their share; the weaker, the great majority, fail to obtain it and perish. *Many are called but few are chosen.* Thus, as generation after generation passes away, the strongest—or, it may be, not the strongest always, but the fittest—survive, while the less fit are eliminated by the severity of the competition for existence, being destroyed by starvation, by climate, by disease, or by the stronger animals. In this way each generation, developing what we will for the present call those *accidental* variations in the individual which may happen to be favourable to successful competition, and destroying unfavourable variations, becomes better and better fitted to contend with the peculiar difficulties of its environments. Different environments call out and develop different fitnesses, different faculties, exercising and developing some organs, repressing and destroying others. Hence arise differences of kind in the same species, and hence also—it is suggested—arise still greater differences, so great as to constitute difference of species itself.

Call this complex system Nature, and even the man of science must confess that Nature wears here her sternest aspect. Call it God, call it the work of Him whose name is Love: and there is at once felt to be something more than sternness. It is as though the Creator, dismissing His creatures fresh from His hands upon their paths of life, had said to them: *Be fruitful and multiply; replenish the earth—and be subdued and perish in the work of replenishment: be fruitful past the bounds of nature, and multiply to your own destruction.*

Can this be God's law? Strength may be wonderful and swiftness wonderful: but, that the strength of the lion should be developed by the ferocity of pursuit, and that the swiftness of the gazelle should be developed by the agonizing dread of capture repeated thousands of times in a single life, this is more fearful than wonderful. Again, instinct also is wonderful. When the bird scarcely a week old beats against its cage in alarm, because it hears the cry of the hawk, whom it has never seen and of whose destructive powers it has had no experience—testifying, as it seems to testify, to a traditional store of hereditary terror, and leading us back to imagine how many millions of agonizing fears must have been endured by that bird's ancestors before such a legacy of instinctive dread could have been accumulated—this instinctive act is wonderful, most wonderful: but it is also most fearful. Can we give thanks to God for this wonderful fear? Can we say here also, with the Psalmist, *I will praise thee; for it is fearfully and wonderfully made?*

Yes, we can praise God, we illogical Christians, we who believe in a Supreme Good but also believe in an ever-resisting, ever-receding Evil. The agony and the ferocity, we say, come from evil. *An enemy hath done this.* The swiftness, the beauty, the strength, the development of every faculty in every living thing—this, we say, comes from the Author of good, who, as the years roll on, is manifesting more and more His triumph over evil.

Logical persons may reject our solution, or rather our cutting of the knot: but even they can scarcely deny that the destruction of life by living creatures presents less difficulties now than it did before it had received the recent light of science. As long as we had before our eyes only one or two pages of this terrible record of destruction—waste everywhere, death everywhere, and development nowhere—at least nowhere plainly legible because incapable of being plainly manifested in so narrow a compass—the problem was most bewildering, and we could do little but acknowledge the difficulty, and say with Bishop Butler, that we saw but a part of the plan, and that if more of the plan were revealed, the difficulty might possibly be diminished or removed. But, now that geology has thrown open to us scores and hundreds of fresh pages, the purpose of the book of creation is clearer. Death is traced throughout the volume as an evil, but as an evil that is being subordinated to development and progress.

The name of that great theologian, the author of the *Analogy of Religion*, emboldens me to make a protest against a common assumption that greatly increases the strain laid upon our faith by the phenomena of death. It is assumed, as a matter of course, by many educated as well as by uneducated persons that there is no second state for any animals below the human race. If this be so, then, indeed, the spectacle of the infinite waste of life must be fraught with additional perplexity. But if it is not so,—and Bishop Butler soberly but most distinctly protests against the assumption that it is so—if for the lower creatures, as well as for man, there are destined future states, life upon life, rising in the scale of development—from inorganic to organic life, and from the lower to the higher organisms—then almost all the horror now excited by the thought of the waste of animal life, is at once felt to be possibly superfluous. For then, as among men, so among the lower animals, the experience of death, as well as the experience of life, may be a part of the preparation for a higher state, and all those lower experiences, those fears and agonies, may be the germs of higher experiences, of nobler fears, and purer pains, moulding and shaping each creature till it is at last conformed to its divine ideal, and the poet's hope may at last be found to have been realised :—

> *That not a worm is cloven in vain,*
> *That not a moth with vain desire,*
> *Is shrivel'd in a fruitless fire,*
> *Or but subserves another's gain.*

Verily, if this be true, then, in spite of pain and death, we may still say, with the Psalmist, *The glory of the Lord shall endure for ever: the Lord shall rejoice in His works.*

You see, as we look into this "natural selection," there are found more and more aspects of it that would justify us in calling it a "divine selection." The conflict for existence is found to be more than a chance *mêlée*—giving the conquest to vulgar force. If it were not for the "variations" in the individuals of each race, no amount of mere conflict could produce development. Whence came these "variations?" Science has scarcely as yet supplied a full answer to that question; yet this principle of "variation" is no less important than that of competition. In some sense it is more important; for "variation" supplies the materials from which competition selects. The principle of conflict is— at least it must be so to us—an imperfect, an evil principle; but it is forced to beneficial results by the intervening principle of "variation" and also by the restricting barriers of Nature. It is as though an evil principle communicating an evil impulse to the first created germ had propelled it into space, blindly rushing into self-destruction; but at each point in the line of motion steps in a counter-law, a law of attraction towards a divine focus, so that as the joint resultant of these two contending motions there issues the symmetrical ellipse, which, in the course of ages—when Good absorbs Evil and becomes the centre of existence—is to orb into the perfect circle.

But, another law of God (beside the principle of variation), has been at work modifying what is called natural selection. This law has been to some extent antagonistic to the law of conflict. The law of conflict may be called the survival of the strongest or fittest: but this other is the survival of the most beautiful. Beauty of shape and colour, the charm of song and the fascination of varied plumage, these qualities, we are told, have exercised an effectual influence in securing the propagation of the more beautiful forms of nature, in spite of their weakness; and in repressing deformed strength and powerful ugliness.

And is this less a divine work because the Divine Master has made His creatures instrumental to it? Are we the less justified in supposing that God loves beauty because we find that he has been making all beautiful objects by first teaching His creatures to love beauty? Has the Creator the less credit (to speak as a man) for his painting of the plumage of the peacock, or for the song of the soaring lark, because every spot and gleam in that plumage, and every note in that flood of melody, are the results of the accumulated delight of countless generations of His creatures? *Consider the lilies of the field how they grow. They toil not neither do they spin: and yet I say unto you that Solomon in all his glory was not arrayed like one of these.* So spoke the Son of God; He whose spirit taught men a lesson not taught by the great poets and artists of Greece or Rome—to regard with affection the beauty of even the apparent inutilities of nature. Well, consider the lilies of the field: what has science to say as to the manner in which God has clothed them? Science tells us that the clothing of the flower, like everything else that is good and beautiful in nature, has been fashioned by many ages of development. Moreover she adds that her story of the flowers must needs be incomplete unless she is allowed to speak of the insects also. Insects, linked with flowers by a connection long unsuspected, have not only fertilised the flowers, but also, discerning the brighter flowers in each species more easily than the less bright, have fertilised the former to the neglect of the latter, and thus, acquiring an instinctive attraction towards colour, have helped to make the fields more bright and more beautiful in each age than in the ages gone before. Each speck and spot in each petal of each flower bears witness to the labours of those creatures whom, for ages, until science taught us the truth, we had been in the habit of treating as proverbial emblems of beautiful idleness. Thus has God clothed the grass of the field, year by year, with increasing glory; and surely He is none the less the author of this glory, because He has wrought it through the joyful labours of His obedient creatures.

It would be possible to mention other cases where geology, so far from diminishing, rather increases the reasonableness of our trust in a beneficent Creator. For example, the earthquakes that swallow whole cities at a time are revealed by science as mysteries still, but mysterious results of the supporting causes that prevent the earth's crust from becoming a level ocean-bed. Again, if we are inclined to speak lightly of modern waste, we are reminded of the ages of apparent waste when layer upon layer of generations after generations of forest-trees were being accumulated by Nature, destined hereafter to be our stores of fuel. Other instances of the same kind may possibly occur to you: but it is time to quit detail and to pass to our conclusion.

And our conclusion is, not indeed that the highest attributes of God are or can be demonstrated for us by science—for that we are agreed cannot and ought not to be—but that science does help those who believe in God to believe in God more reasonably. Apparent waste, and pain, and lavish death are found of old as they are found now: but the waste is in some cases proved to be apparent and not real; the pain is found to conduce to the development of new instincts or faculties; death is found to be the condition of higher life; beauty is found to be an unsuspected power in the world; evil is indeed found mixed with good, then as now, and even more then than now—evil with good, and ugliness with beauty—but beauty, from the first triumphing over ugliness, and evil more and more subordinated to good.

Evil is subordinated to good. "But," it may be replied, "is not good also subordinated to evil? Is it not true that, in proportion as an animal rises in the scale of creation, in that proportion he becomes capable of wider aberration from the laws of Nature? Does not increase of faculty and of freedom imply increase of fault?"

Yes, it implies increase of fault, but increase of virtue also, and we believe that the fault is subordinated to virtue, the evil to good. Go back to the lowest forms of animal life and pass upward from these to the highest: begin from the submarine creatures, the sea-anemones, the sponges, and the like—more vegetable than animal—whether using their animal faculty of motion or helplessly swaying with the swaying tide one can scarcely tell—and compare these animated vegetables, these incipiently living plants, with the dog, the companion of man. Only imagine the absurdity of applying to the former such epithets as we habitually apply to the latter—sagacious, obedient, brave, gentle, faithful. How vast the superiority of the latter in faculties, in freedom, and in potential virtue. Yet it is not to be denied that with the possibility of all these virtues comes the possibility of corresponding faults—I had almost committed the anachronism of saying *sins:* but sin is reserved for man, and man is not yet created.

"So then, it seems, the result of all these ages of preparation, of conflict overruled to development, of agony transmuted into a basis of instinct —the result of all this Divine guidance is to increase the possibility of error." Thus we might have reasoned, had we been witnesses of these primeval times, and we might have added a prediction that "if the Creator is planning the evolution of some still higher being than as yet exists, a being endowed with still higher faculties and greater freedom of action, then we must anticipate a greater depth of error than any yet experienced: and the result of this fresh exaltation will be an abysmal fall."

Our answer to all this is that, according to our belief and hope, although evil apparently increases in the subtlety and power of its temptations as God's creatures rise, yet this apparent increase of evil will only serve to *make evil exceeding evil*, to manifest it in its highest form of evil, in order that it may meet its most complete extinction. Increase as evil may, who would not sooner be a man with all man's faculties for sin, than a sponge with faculties for almost nothing, good or bad? To comprehend this mystery of sin will always be impossible, and to aim at comprehension is puerile; but is it not possible, and if possible, is it not helpful to trace some thread of purpose, visible even to us blear-eyed mortals, and running through the whole of creation? May it not have been, from the very first, God's will that all, even the humblest members of the animal world, should owe their development partly to Him and His servant the material world, but partly also to some motion, some action, some effort, some exercise of will, of their own?

The lowest creatures are acted on by the direct impulse of Nature; they expand or contract, sway this way or that, under the pressure of the waters or the touch of passing particles; their approximation to free will is little more than self-motion, and error with them is scarcely conceivable. As creation rises in the scale, a succession of actions under impulse is found to have generated in higher creatures an instinctive habit, to which they are often blindly subservient, but their subservience to it has emancipated them from the lower slavery to mere direct impulse; ferocity and gentleness, cunning and skill, can sometimes be predicated of individuals; their developed faculties and increased freedom have given them something approaching to free-will, something approaching to moral and immoral action. Lastly, among the highest of all, such as the dog and the elephant, varied instincts seem so to balance one another as almost to have originated a new controlling power, a germ of understanding; social instincts have given rise to something more than ordinary instinctive affection: on the other hand in these highest creatures there appear possibilities of viciousness and derangement such as are not found in lower animals. Now throughout this series of organisms does it not seem that, although evil appears more prominently in each higher phase, yet, on the whole, the good is proportionately more prominent? Does not there seem, on the whole, traceable throughout, from the polypus to the dog, discernible even in what we call "the brute" creation, something like a purpose of preparing the way for moral goodness; and to this preparation does not the increased development of moral evil appear to be subordinate?

Brethren, what shall we say of God's animal world, described to us by science as thus *fearfully and wonderfully made?* Shall we glorify Him the less, because He has never changed His mind; because His works, based on eternal laws, exhibit a continuous progress? What is there to be alarmed at here? Is there anything frightful in the phrase "the eternal laws of God?" Then say instead, and perhaps more truthfully, "the eternal will of God," who, in the primeval records of earth, is thus exhibited to us as shaping a human will out of brute impulse and instinct, in order to prepare the way for that supreme sacrifice of the human will to the Divine, foreordained before the foundation of the world, for the purpose of conforming man to God. What answer shall we make to such a dream or suggestion or revelation of science? Brethren, let us make answer in words familiar to us all, glorifying God because, in the midst of change, He is the same, and, in spite of resistance, His Will is unchangeable: *As it was in the beginning is now and ever shall be, world without end. Glory be to the Father, and to the Son, and to the Holy Ghost.*

FAITH AND SCIENCE.

III.—THE CREATION OF MAN.

I will praise thee, for I am fearfully and wonderfully made; marvellous are thy works, and that my soul knoweth right well.—PSALM cxxxix. 14.

THE subject of the Creation of Man naturally suggests the account of it given in the earlier chapters of the Book of Genesis. Regarded unscientifically, as the utterances of men divinely inspired to proclaim, in the earliest times, a God of order and progress, who made man in His image, and intends to make man after His likeness, these chapters will always claim our most reverent attention: but to attempt to treat them as scientific treatises anticipating, in language of scientific accuracy, the modern discoveries of astronomy, geology, and physiology, would be a mistake. This is now, I believe, recognized by all educated men. The Speaker's Commentary on the Bible—which I quote as exhibiting in its highest legitimate development that charitable caution which should always be used in dealing

with the popular conceptions of religion—commenting on the account of the creation of the sun and moon on the fourth day, after the creation of the light, the firmament, the land and sea, and vegetation, makes the following remark:—
"The narrative only tells us what sun, moon, and stars are in relation to the earth." These words, with slight modification will, I think, apply to the whole of the narrative of the Creation. But I should omit the word "only" and should say, "This narrative tells us what the Universe was in relation to an earthly observer, inspired by the Creator to proclaim in very early times that there had been order and progress in Creation from the beginning to the making of Man after God's image."

This is not the view that was taken of these chapters in centuries gone by. Then they were generally regarded as being scientifically and literally accurate; now they cannot be thus regarded. But I think that, so far from being disquieted, we ought to be grateful if the lapse of centuries has taught us a truer appreciation of the Scriptures; and we ought hopefully to anticipate that further lapse of time will throw yet fuller light on every page of Holy Writ. Nay more, as we are now trained in these times by God's fuller revelation of His material works, I think many of us would feel a certain sense of something unfit and almost grotesque, in the notion that a law of Science, not to be discovered intellectually for thousands of years afterwards, should be unconsciously promulgated by a writer under the influence of divine inspiration. If, for example, the author of the hundred-and-fourth Psalm, while describing the Almighty as *clothing Himself with light as with a garment*, had uttered words unintelligible to his audience at the time, but intelligible to us now, as containing the secret expression of some law of light quite recently discovered; or, to take another instance, if, in the impassioned and highly poetic description of the battle of Beth-horon, the writer had been moved to say, not that *the sun stood still* but that "the earth stood still," should we not feel (quite independently of our knowledge that the earth could not possibly have stood still) a certain painful sense of intellectual waste and of incongruity in the casual, unconscious, and unused prediction of an astronomical discovery destined to remain for many centuries unknown to mankind? Surely it is far better for us, and certainly it is far more truthful, to recognize that the object of the Bible is to set forth a spiritual revelation of God, and that our religion does not stand or fall with the scientific accuracy or inaccuracy of any cosmogonic theory.

Due weight being given to these considerations, we can accept, at least hypothetically, the theories propounded by Science as to the origin and development of man without any faithless perturbation. Whether the details of the creation and the fall of man given in the Book of Genesis be allegorical, or whatever other explanation of them may ultimately be adopted, the solid groundwork of spiritual revelation, that God made man according to His image and intends to make man according to His likeness, will be always precious, always divine.

You may have observed that I have twice distinguished between the "image" and the "likeness," the past creation and the future intention of the Creator. Where one is uncertain as to the exact meaning of an author, it is frivolous and almost dishonest to base elaborate theories upon a word or phrase. Still, it has always seemed to me that there is something very suggestive in the distinction drawn by Origen between these two words "image" and "likeness."[1] It might seem to an English reader that the word "image" implies a stronger resemblance than the word "likeness;" but this opinion would not, I believe, be justified by the original Hebrew, nor is it the interpretation adopted by Origen. God made man according to His image, that is to say, with a certain degree of resemblance to Himself, and He intended and intends to make man according to His likeness. *Let us make man in our image, after our likeness*—that was the intention. But the Bible goes on to describe only the first part of the intention as being fulfilled; *so God created man in His own image;* but, adds

[1] Origen was not the first to draw this distinction. See *Clem. Alex. Stromata*, ii. 22, 132.

Origen, "not as yet after His likeness." That was to be the work of centuries. Man was made from the first in the *image* of God with divine potentialities of reason and love, but ages were needed and will yet be needed before these potentialities shall become realities and man shall be conformed in all respects to the divine *likeness*. I repeat that I do not use this view of Origen as an argument, but rather as a suggestive illustration. Viewed as an illustration it suggests progress, it suggests development, and seems to prepare the way for the scientific theory, which we are now to consider.

But before passing to this theory, let me remind you of our position. We are not here to discuss the probability, still less to criticize the accuracy of scientific theories; we have no pretensions to do so, and, if it were possible, this would not be the place or time to do it. We are here to-day in the capacity of moderately educated Christians, with just enough of knowledge to understand an untechnical exposition of scientific theory, and just enough intelligence to distinguish between a scientific theory and a theological inference. We are oppressed with the atmosphere of religious distrust; wearied with the exultant prating that this or that new theory is to be proved indubitably true, and, as its consequence, is to overthrow the faith of Christ; saddened at the spectacle of thousands of our countrymen wistfully turning now to Theology, now to Science, while they oscillate from belief to unbelief under the impulse of this scientific treatise or that theological refutation, everyone craving for certainty and crying " Only give us certainty ; is there a Christ, or is there not ?" We feel that such faithlessness, such oscillation, is likely to paralyse us for all good useful work in life: and we ask, " Is it possible that faith in Christ can be of such a nature as to be shaken by the unearthing of a new fossil or the discovery of an Uncial Manuscript ? Will it not be well that, before plunging into the absorbing work of active life, as clergymen, as physicians, as barristers, we should endeavour to look these questions fairly in the face, up here, at the University, where there are many whose pleasure as well as avowed duty it is to help us to remain loyal to the Truth, and therefore to Christ." That is the way in which I regard your position, and I put it to you, is it not better for you to consider these difficulties first with friends, before you hear them, as you assuredly will, from the antagonists of Christianity ?

For this purpose, I ask you to look forward twenty years or more, and to suppose, for the sake of argument, that in that interval fresh discoveries will demonstrate the truth of much that is at present unproved. My conviction is, that there is nothing either present or impending, either from science or from criticism, that need cause fear to any rational Christian; and, in this conviction, I will beg you to give me your attention while we assume the theory of the development of mankind, at each assumption asking ourselves the question, "Need I cease to be a Christian even supposing this should be proved to be true?"

Science differs from popular religion in asserting that man has, as a rule, progressed and not retrograded. Even Science, as we shall shortly see, will scarcely deny that, in a certain sense, there has been a fall of man; but the fall is subordinated, in the scientific aspect, to the consequent rise; and, on the whole, development is regarded as clearly traceable. On this theory, man was at first destitute of reason and of moral sense, and endowed with instinct alone. By what processes, and at what stage, language was introduced, and instinct so far gave place to reason as to place a gulf between man and all other animals, this question Science would probably confess her inability to answer—at all events in detail and at present. But it is confidently asserted that, as we are now unanimous in acknowledging that the creation of the vegetable and of the animal world was accomplished not suddenly, but by processes prolonged for many ages of ages, so we ought to believe that the shaping and moulding of man from lower stages of being until he was elaborated to his present form, was not the sudden work of a moment or of a day, but the gradual result of many progressive generations.

In virtue of what faculty did man rise from his lower level, and become what he is? Science will answer, in virtue of the faculty of *attention*—a faculty of receiving impressions more forcibly and retaining them more tenaciously than other animals. To the lower creatures incidents present themselves as isolated incidents; the past is forgotten or only indefinitely retained in the residuum of an instinctive habit: but to man was communicated by Nature, acting according to her laws of selection, the power of retaining the past and grouping it with the present. Hence came a habit of classifying and comparing, and from this great faculty of comparing came the very names of *man* and *mind*. *Man* is the comparing creature, and *mind* means the comparing power. The polypus is the servant of present and direct impulse; the higher animals also are under the dominion of the pressing instinct of the moment—both under the tyranny of the present: but man was enabled, by comparing the present with the past, to emancipate himself from the tyranny of the present, and, once emancipated, it was a natural step for him to push forward into the future. All these faculties were developed and strengthened by the conflict for existence; and thus, out of the seed of *attention*, sprang, first Memory, called by the Greek poet *the industrious mother of all things*, and, after Memory, Forethought.

Nature must have seemed hard and cruel to some of those early races. (I assume their existence, and shall not again think it necessary to remind you that we are dealing with possibilities or probabilities, and not with absolutely proved facts.) With no weapons for the chase except their nets, with no knowledge of metals, nothing but sharpened flints to serve as spear-heads or as knives, disputing with the wild beasts the possession of their caves, with none of the comforts or ornaments or certainties of modern life,—the gift of forethought must have seemed to them indeed a doubtful gift, bringing with it as much pain as consolation, the forethought of to-morrow's starvation, of to-morrow's destruction. Yet, in reality, the pressure of nature was sharpening their inventive and reasoning faculties, as well as developing their physical powers. The conflict for existence was eliminating the weakly and the feeble, but it also eliminated the improvident and thoughtless. Already the victory was not always to the strong. Wisdom or cunning was becoming a power in the world. Thus, if Memory was rightly called by the Greek poet the Mother, it is no less true that Necessity was the Father of all human invention.

Meantime, other besides intellectual qualities were being developed in man. Again etymology [1] comes to the aid of history and suggests that, in that language which was the common origin of our and other kindred languages, Memory is closely connected with a moral faculty, the highest of all faculties, that by which we approach God Himself,

[1] Max Müller's "Lectures on the Science of Language," vol. i. p. 435.

the faculty of love. Nor is the connection difficult to discern. Without memory, without the recollection of these incidents on which is based the gratitude of the child to the parents and the permanent interest of parents in children, filial love could rise to nothing higher than the transitory instinct that appears to unite parents and offspring in the majority of animals. Hence Memory, the *mother of all things*, introduced a new and higher feeling of affection, differing altogether from the mere social instinct that leads some of the higher animals to co-operate together for the common good. Doubtless science would assert that for many ages the affection of the human family differed but little, as it still differs little in some barbarous tribes, from animal instinct; still, the impulse to permanence once being given, and being encouraged, in the conflict for existence, by the resulting advantage derived by the united family in contending against the difficulties of their environment, the ultimate result was that definite enduring feeling of attachment to which we give the name of love.

Of all natural influences, this, the training of family affection, must have been indeed the most potent in conforming man to God. Wherever the *two or three* of the human family have been gathered together throughout the world, there, sometimes undeveloped, suppressed too often, but still potentially existent, there has been God's Spirit of Love that lighteth every man that cometh into the world: and in virtue of this faculty, this power of loving, as distinct from the mere attraction of animal instinct, man differs from all other creatures, and may be said to be in the image of Him whose name is Love.

The principle of union, having once obtained a footing, extended itself from the family to the connections of the families, from a group of families to a tribe. In the struggle for existence, union was found an advantage, often more than compensating for want of strength and cunning. Those tribes that could combine more readily and closely than others, began, as a rule, to assert their superiority. Union for self-defence against the common enemy, strengthened the tie that bound the tribe together, and widened the field for the development of social virtue. And thus it came to pass that, even among the most savage tribes, tribes ignorant perhaps of the name and notion of a God, and unable to calculate even to the number of their fingers, yet even there, unsung by any poet, arose the feeling of patriotism, and it was found *sweet and honourable to die for one's country*.

Union was caused by fear. The dread of wild beasts may have done much towards forcing men together, but the dread of men probably did more. Thus out of evil arose good. The greediness and violence of mankind compelled men to unite, and, within the narrow limits of their union, to refrain from greediness and violence towards each other. Moreover union required something more from the tribesmen than the mere abstinence from injuring his fellows. Union in war implies obedience and discipline; union in peace implies law.

And now, with the introduction of law, had come the time for the revelation of sin. Although, as a rule, whatever a strong man had done had hitherto caused no repulsion, and whatever a weak man had done had caused contempt, yet already there had crept in exceptions to this rule, and these exceptions were on the increase. True, law did not extend beyond the limits of one's tribe; to pity an enemy was weak and contemptible, to carry off an enemy's cattle, or lay waste his land, or enslave his family, or destroy his life— this was strong and useful to the tribe and therefore good. But, within the limits of the tribe, law was a strong controlling power: to slay or enslave or injure those of one's own tribe, this was obviously not useful, this was harmful to the tribe. By degrees, as custom hardened into law, all violations of law, independently of their public harmfulness (which sometimes might not be obvious) came to seem shocking. They were not only harmful, they were not only unusual; they were bad. Not even a hero's strength could make them seem good. Such actions were often visited by vengeance. The offender was excluded from the society of the tribe, or fined or dishonoured; or, if not punished, yet made painfully aware that he had estranged his tribe by breaking the tribe's law, and that, at any moment, vengeance for the broken law might descend upon his head.

Hence sprang a new sense of uneasiness, a new and bitter recognition of a higher rule than that of impulse. The impulse to indulge one's thirst for vengeance was strong, and the indulgence pleasant; but the after-thought was painful, and the pain was greater than the pleasure. A beast of the field might have forgotten the past in bondage to the present: but a man, with a man's painful privilege of memory, could not forget, but must remember against his will. And thus, recalling the past pleasure, and comparing it with the present greater pain, and realising also the usefulness and majesty of the Law he had broken, and the mischief that he had brought upon his tribe, the transgressor felt that the impulse to obey Law was better, and ought to have been stronger, than the impulse to obey pleasure. He had done what was not useful, he had worked harm, but he had done more than that—he had violated Law. A strange unsilenceable voice within him testified to the violation, and this voice was Conscience.

Sometimes the law of the tribe was, in the main, in accordance with the laws of Nature, and, in such cases, conscience would testify more directly to a controlling Justice. At other times the law of a tribe might be perverted from Nature; it might inculcate evil, might repress good. Then the conscience also would be perverted, and while condemning some things that were good, would approve some things that were evil. But, in almost all cases, the law of the tribe contained some reflection of the Supreme Law; and, in that degree, the conscience testified not merely to the imperfect law of this or that tribe but to a higher law not yet fully revealed.

Whence came this mysterious law, this strange invisible power that made the strong abstain from injuring the weak, and compelled the many to obey the few? the power that curbed the proud and delighted to avenge itself on the bloodthirsty; that dogged men with fears in their waking hours, and refused to be excluded even when the eyes were closed in sleep? Whence came those terrible shapes that haunted them in the darkness, when the familiar forms of earthly things could not be discerned? They could not be seen by day, therefore they were not of earth; they came by night, like the shadowy shapes of their forefathers from some place of their own. As the breath vanishes in the air, so vanished these shapes in the light of the day; they must be Breaths or Spirits.

As the law rose, man fell. *Without the law sin was dead. For I was alive without the law once: but, when the commandment came, sin revived and I died. And the commandment which was ordained to life, I found to be unto death.* These words of St. Paul exactly describe the change that befalls the human mind, passing from ignorance to the knowledge of good and evil. Such a change has been experienced by every one of you more than once in your lives, and has yet, I trust, to be experienced before your lives are ended. The passage from infancy to childhood, from childhood to youth, from youth to manhood, and from stage to stage of subsequent maturity and decline, brings its new knowledge of good and evil, its new and higher standard of conduct, and, consequently—since the ideal is always in advance of the actual—its new sin or fall. And such a fall must there have been when humanity awoke to the knowledge of a higher will or law than the law of self-will or impulse. Before the introduction of law, man may have obeyed his instincts, like the beasts of the field, without uneasiness or repentance; when the higher law was introduced, this was no longer possible. The bliss of ignorance departed for ever, leaving, instead, a very painful wisdom, destructive of past complacency and of the old unreflecting contentment.

From henceforth man felt that he and Nature were at strife. Before, Nature and he had been friends, or at all events not enemies; he had obeyed Instinct, the law of his being, and had, so far, been in harmony with Nature. Now he and Nature were out of harmony. His will was against Nature. Conscious of his newly-acquired faculty of will, he attributed the same faculty to his new enemy. The will of Nature was against his. Personified by the fears of a guilty conscience, Nature assumed the aspect of a foe, an avenger. Before, in the old times, before the curse had fallen, he had known want and failure, but not resistance, not opposition. Before, he had been unsuccessful in the chase, or overtaken by night in the forest, or his cave had been inundated by the rising river; but all this had been a part of the law of his life, there had been no sense of hostility, scarcely of hardship. But now all was changed. Nature had turned against him. If he was unsuccessful now in fishing or hunting, it was because the winds had betrayed him, or the roughening waves refused to aid him, or the all-seeing Sun had betrayed his secret, or the unkind Moon had veiled her face in clouds. The very air that he breathed now rebelled against him, sending pinching cold and fog and rain; the very ground on which he trod turned a traitor, and brought forth thorns and thistles, instead of fruits. Verily, the earth was cursed for his sake.

Now comes Religion into the field—Religion, the art of bribing Spirits, for thus it must be regarded in its lower aspect—the knowledge of charms and incantations, of the caprices of Evil Beings, and of the sacrifices necessary to appease and conciliate them;—Religion, so forcibly described by the great Latin poet as trampling human life beneath the weight of its foul oppression, the mother of wicked and impious deeds. And certainly the thought of all that has been done, and among some savage tribes is still being done, in the name of Religion, might seem to justify the poet's condemnation. The worship of stocks and stones, of gods of rag or straw, to be threatened and coaxed, rewarded and punished; the abstinence from nature's common gifts; the self-torture, and self-mutilation; the gloom of servile dread blackening all human life,—all this is but the degrading aspect of Religion; but, when we turn to its immoral aspect, to the sacrifice of life, of purity, of parental love, then indeed, bewildered by the thought of so many butcheries perpetrated in religion's name, horrified by the shrieks of innocent children beneath the sacrificial knife or in the fiery embrace of conciliated gods, we may well cry with Lucretius, *Alas, Religion! How hast thou tempted men to evil!*

Yet religion was an advance; and step by step the Fall was preparing the way for Redemption. To some it might seem that, rather than be cursed with such a parody of true religion, it would have been better to have had no religion at all. Man, with face erect, capable of will, capable of love, endowed with memory, endowed with reason, yet howling with his fellows, self-lacerated, around an idol reeking with his children's blood, compared with the dog by his side, might seem a retrograding, a lower animal. But it was not so. The notion of an external and more powerful will than that of man, was a gain. The evil consisted in man's attempt to conform the external Will to himself, instead of himself to the Will. By many failures he was to be taught that he must not make God in his own image, but must yield himself to be conformed to the image of God.

Very slow and stubborn have men been, at the best, in learning this lesson of divine conformity —some races slower than others. Waste is not absent from the human world, any more than from the world of animal and vegetable existence. Some tribes there are, even now, that regard God as an evil rather than a good—a Being to be destroyed if possible, but, if not to be destroyed, then to be conciliated and bribed; others there are that seem not as yet to have attained even to the notion of a God. A painful and bewildering spectacle! But not so bewildering, I think, upon the supposition that these tribes have been slower than others in learning the progressive lessons of existence, as upon the popular supposition that, from a perfect intellectual and moral condition, they have been reduced to a state in which they have no words to count the number of their fingers, or to express the ideas of purity, of love, of goodness, of God.

Natural selection prepared the way for a truer theology by discouraging the lower types of religion. In the conflict for existence, the race that was hampered by the lower religion contended at a disadvantage with the race that had attained to the higher religion. Of course I do not mean to assert that, in all cases, the higher religion prevailed over the lower. There are other causes of national conquest beside the religious element; and there are many instances to show that strength, ferocity, and discipline, however superstitious, may prevail, for a time, over a more intelligent and more moral race. But, other things being equal, superstition was a disadvantage. It paralysed the intellect, imbuing its victims with hopelessness and lethargy. It made itself felt as a disadvantage not only in the war of race against race, but also in the struggle against the inclemency of nature. The man that could believe in a good spirit was, other things being equal, at an advantage as compared with the man that could believe in none but bad spirits.

The arts of life prepared the way for theology. The art of sharpening a flint-stone led to an improvement in the weapons of man. Improved weapons delivered him to some extent from the dread of wild beasts. Inconceivable to us is the change that must have been thus wrought in human nature. Historians tell us that, in ancient times, whole tribes occasionally perished, exterminated by wild beasts. Try to imagine this: a collection of human beings, endowed with reason, striving for a generation, perhaps for generations, against the unreasoning brute force in the surrounding forests, and being worsted in the contest. For a creature—reasonable or capable of reason though he may be—who has seen his parents, children, brothers, sisters, wife, carried off by the monsters of the jungle, or torn and devoured before his eyes, while he, the helpless witness of their agonies and shrieks, lives in perpetual dread that to-morrow will bring the same fate upon himself—how is it possible that, in such an atmosphere of horrid dread, there could be a breath of hope or faith in the existence of a Supreme Good? It is not possible. Such a perfection of fear must have cast out all thought of the love of any spirit. If any thought of Deity at all could enter the hearts of men contending with beasts, on equal or inferior terms, force and cruelty must have been deified as the dominating principle of the jungle. But, when men attained, by art, an increasing superiority over their savage enemies, then they had breathing-space and leisure for hope, and hopeful thoughts about a helpful spirit. And thus the art of sharpening a flint-stone prepared the way for theology.

Other arts were invented. Metals were discovered and utilised. Trees were felled, forests cleared; the beasts, once so formidable, had been destroyed or forced to flee from the neighbourhood of man. The wheat-field—that great divine test of patient faithful work, taxing and developing man's forethought and perseverance and trust in the regular processes of nature—became a novelty, a custom, a necessity; and with the patient tilling of the field came, first a temporary sacrifice of a hunter's wandering life, and then the toleration, and at last the love, of a fixed home. The sound of music began to be heard among the villages, suggesting other and higher harmonies than those of sound; and when the labour of the harvest was over, the husbandman, enfranchised from precarious dependence upon the daily chase, and led by settled life toward thoughts more deep and connected than the unstable and isolated fancies of a hunter's wanderings, found leisure to sit down and ask himself, "Whence come seed-time and harvest? Who sends the sun to ripen our corn? Who banishes him to his evening darkness and calls him back each morning? What Being is it that commands the blade to spring up, and the green ear to become golden, and gives the ripe corn to men? Whatever Being it may be, He must needs be good and kind." And thus again the arts of life prepared the way for theology.

But even this improved theology was very imperfect. Men had not yet attained to the notion of the One Perfect Will. It was a great step upward to have conceived that the invisible wills—the spirits that controlled or identified themselves with earth and air and sea—were good spirits; still, plurality of wills implied possible conflict; conflict implied inferiority in one of the two combatants; inferiority implied imperfection. Therefore men's theology was imperfect. So indeed our Christian theology is, regarded logically; for we too believe in a conflict between good and evil. But the theology of antiquity believed in a conflict between good spirits; and that was fatal to its permanence.

At this point, if not before this point, we have passed out of prehistoric times; and I ought, before this, to have asked you the question we have to ask ourselves—"Is there anything in all this that need make us cease to believe in Christ?" One is tempted by a sense of continuity to encroach on the historic periods and to attempt to trace, at least in the familiar histories of Greece and Rome, the continued development of mankind by natural selection. But we must pass to the central event in human history, the coming of Christ.

Each phase of Selection had done its work. By giving the victory in the conflict for existence, to the strong, to the cunning, the wise, the patriotic, Selection had strengthened the bodies and the minds of men. Eastern obedience, Greek skill and discipline, Roman order and reverence for law, all these national virtues had been tried, and the nations embodying them had been brought, each in turn, to the front; but all these had been found unequal to the task of continuing the progress of humanity, and of conforming man to God.

Now, therefore, a new phase of Selection was at hand: a Selection at once Natural and Divine—a selection of the weakest, the humblest, the most unselfish; this was to be the new conquering race to survive in the Survival of the Fittest. And in this solemn Manifesto the Sovereign of the new Kingdom proclaimed the passing away of the old Natural Selection and the introduction of the new Selection of God:—*The kings of the Gentiles exercise lordship over them; and they that exercise authority upon them are called benefactors. But ye shall not be so: but he that is greatest among you, let him be as the younger; and he that is chief, as he that doth serve.*

Thus, then, at the very moment when the final fall of man seemed imminent, the Uplifting came. Just when the image of God in mankind seemed to be in danger of being irreparably defaced, it was found that God was but effacing a part of the human image in order to conform the human to the divine. What if the work of Christ is still incomplete, still barely begun? To us, who worship Christ as the Son of God, to us who look upon Christ's life on earth as the central event of all the ages of this earth's existence, what can there seem unreasonable in supposing that a score or two of centuries may be yet required before mankind can approximate to His level, and the work of His Spirit can be accomplished?

Nevertheless the new age has already begun, and Christ's new principle of selection is henceforth to be supreme. Not force now, nor skill, nor wisdom, nor discipline; but love, and love alone, is to be the ruling law of the world. Henceforth all the operations of natural selection are to be naturally reversed: *Blessed are the meek, for they shall inherit the earth.* Old things are passed away, behold, all things are become new. The Spirit of Christ, that is, the spirit of love, is naturally to supplant the old competitive spirit, and to become, as it were, the new environment of man. Pity is to become as natural as once was vengeance. Sin is to be hated—sin, but not sinners;—and sin itself is to be ultimately extinguished by love. The hampering bounds of nations are to be broken. The whole world is to be one family of brothers, looking up, through Christ, the Elder Brother of mankind, to God the Father of all. The apostles and soldiers of this faith are to be the conquerors of the world, smiting evil with their two-edged sword, and breaking it to pieces like a potter's vessel. Such is the new conquering race brought to the front by the Struggle for Existence, the Survival of the Fittest, the Law of Natural Selection merged in the law — equally natural — of Divine Selection, and ultimately to be called the law of the Divine all-embracing Inclusion.

Brethren, *what shall we say to these things? If God be for us, who can be against us?* What is there, absolutely destructive of all Christian faith, in the supposition that the *fearful and wonderful work* of the creation of man was not completed in twenty-four hours, but in twenty-four ages—say, in twenty-four thousand centuries? What can you see in all this that threatens to separate us from the love of Christ? I can see nothing of the kind. On the contrary there is much that suggests fresh faith and hope. Does mankind seem less likely to be the object of God's care because it is shown that the Creator may possibly have taken a million of years to prepare man's terrestrial home, and another million to fashion his form and to endow him with his god-like faculties? The Maker who has been so fearfully and wonderfully guiding His creatures upwards, through centuries of centuries, in a gradual ascent towards Himself, subordinating death to life, struggle to development, pain to knowledge, and sin itself to righteousness, shall He be thwarted at last in His eternal purpose, or abruptly stop the progress of ages? No, it is not from God's minister, Science, that one need apprehend any fatal antagonism to Christ. Dishonesty and impurity, vindictiveness and malignity, superstition and servility, selfishness and cynicism—these evils may for a time set Our Lord at a distance from us; but as for Truth and Truth's servants, be they what they will, we ought to be able to say in the words of St. Paul that none of these, neither History, nor Criticism, nor Science, nor any Scientific truth whatever, neither Natural Selection nor Theories of Evolution, nor Speculations about Automatism, nor any Pre-historic discoveries present or future, possible or probable, *shall be able to separate us from the love of God which is in Christ Jesus our Lord.*

CHRISTIAN WORK.

And He sent them to preach the kingdom of God, and to heal the sick.—St. Luke ix. 2.

WE are all conscious, not sometimes without a certain uneasiness, that our lives differ considerably from the practice enjoined by many precepts of the New Testament. When we are struck on the right cheek, we do not turn the left to the striker, but take measures that the infringement of the law may be legally punished. We may have food and clothing, and yet we are not contented unless we can also obtain education. We do not always submit ourselves to the powers that be. Instead of giving to every man that asketh of us, we blame indiscriminate almsgiving and constitute beggary a crime.

Further, we are aware that a great part of our existence, all that concerns politics, nearly all that concerns war, much that concerns art, science, commerce, and amusements, is apparently unaffected because unnoticed by the teaching of Christ. To these subjects reference is seldom made from the pulpit; or, if mentioned at all, this vast province of human interests is mostly treated as though it were the land that lieth in darkness and the shadow of death, incapable of being illustrated by the great Light of Christ.

Is there any necessity for this division between the theory and practice of Christians? Let us endeavour to show that there is not. Let us try to prove, or rather to remind one another, that, if we are justified in disobeying the letter of any of the precepts uttered by Christ 1800 years ago, it is because we can hear the voice of Christ dictating to us modern precepts adapted to modern times. In a word, if we are not under a law, not even under a Christian law, it is because we are under a Spirit, and that Spirit the Spirit of Christ.

But it is asserted that there is nothing in Christianity, nor even in Christ Himself, which can answer the questions of modern times. The Christian Code is said to be incomplete, or rather fragmentary; and the same incompleteness is said to characterize the life of Christ. The following are the words of the author of the New Life of Jesus: "Even the life of man in the family is left by the Teacher, Himself childless, in the background: his relation toward the body politic appears simply passive. With trade he is, not only by reason of his calling, unconcerned, but even visibly averse to it; and everything relating to art and the enjoyment of the elegancies of life is absolutely removed from his range of view."

Now there can be no doubt that many of these statements are correct. In the ordinary sense of the word *code*, there is no Christian code at all. Probably all the words of Christ on record might be compressed into a closely printed column of the *Times*. Of His recorded sayings many were evidently, and some probably, intended by Him to apply to special circumstances or particular persons. Take, for instance, the injunction to the apostles, when sent on their missionary journey, to turn their cheeks to the smiter. It has been suggested —and there is great probability in the suggestion —that this command was intended to be obeyed literally at the time. The apostles were going among men ignorant of the new principle of Christian Love, and likely to require the most forcible inculcation before they could conceive of it. Therefore it was to be inculcated in the most forcible of all ways, by action—by a ritual of self-sacrifice, more likely than any words to startle strangers into attention—by courting persecution, welcoming blows, rewarding robbery. Circumstances might easily arise in modern times when the literal obedience to Christ's precept might again become expedient and therefore right. But Christ Himself did not act thus, nor did the Apostle St. Paul. And for a Christian community such a rule seems altogether inapplicable; at least, a very different rule appears to be laid down in the words: *If thy brother shall trespass against thee, go and tell him his fault between thee and him alone . . . but if he will not hear thee then take with thee one or two more, . . . and if he shall neglect to hear them, tell it unto the church; but if he neglect to hear the church, let him be unto thee as an heathen man and a publican.*

Indeed one mysterious passage in St. Luke's Gospel (whatever other meanings it may have) seems expressly to convey the lesson that such "rules of life" as Christ laid down for His disciples must not be supposed to be necessarily permanent: *When I sent you without purse, and scrip, and shoes, lacked ye anything? And they said, Nothing. Then said he unto them, But now, he that hath a purse, let him take it, and likewise his scrip: and he that hath no sword, let him sell his garment and buy one.* But if transientness and non-universal applicability can be predicated of the letter of any one of Christ's rules, then it would seem to follow that new circumstances may at any time arise that may render the letter of the rest transient and non-universally applicable. Hence it must be admitted that—using the word *rules* as distinct from *motives*—we cannot find in the New Testament any universally applicable rules of life.

It must also be admitted that the life of Christ does not (as indeed how could it?) include all the experiences incident to every class, condition, age, and sex of mankind. The artist, the tradesman, the merchant, the politician, will search the gospels in vain for any special prescriptions applicable to their several temptations and moral perplexities.

We must go yet further in our admissions, and confess that even those broad and general questions which present themselves to men in every rank and station of life do not find exact answers in the pages of the New Testament. If, for example, we want to know whether we ought to spend more or to spend less upon ourselves, upon our family, upon the poor: if we are in doubt how far we may legitimately carry the expression of resentment, or to what extent we may be legitimately influenced by affection and gratitude: if we are hesitating between punishing, with the risk of hardening the offender, and forgiving, with the risk of encouraging others to offend; between believing, with the risk of being deceived, and not believing, with the risk of discouraging innocence—it is vain for us to turn to the New Testament as to a Sibylline oracle in the expectation of finding in the sacred pages the exact solution of the moral problem that is perplexing us. Would it be well for us if it were otherwise? Would it tend to the development and culture of mankind that they should possess for the regulation of their lives a great repertory of casuistry wherein was set down every conceivable combination of circumstances with its appropriate action? Would it be well that even a Christian should be absolved from the duty of common sense? Assuredly it would not be well: and were Christianity that complete system of casuistry which sceptics think they want, it would long ago have destroyed all spiritual life, and have proved itself to be that "one good order" which, as the poet says, would "undo the world."

But indeed Christ did not come to construct a Code, but to make men love one another. *By this*, said He, *shall men know that ye are My disciples.* It is true He founded a Kingdom; but the essence of that Kingdom was that it aimed at no Sovereignty but that of Fatherhood, no Citizenship but Brotherhood, no Law but that of Love. The Kingdom of God is a family, and in a family laws are superfluous. Thus Christ's Kingdom is not founded on any code or collection of rules, but on Christ Himself. For this is the great difference between Christ and other lawgivers or teachers, that they legislated, but He *lived*.

Attempts have been made of late to lead us to the inference that Christ taught nothing new, nothing that was not already received as true in His own time by the best of His own nation. We may be inclined to think that such assertions are at least exaggerated: we may be impressed on the one hand by the uncertainty of the date assignable to many Rabbinical precepts, and on the other hand by the extreme rarity of anything approaching to the Christian precepts of universal philanthropy in the pages of the Apocrypha. For, though the theoretic theology of the sublime book called the Wisdom of Solomon maintains that *God loves all things that are, and abhors nothing that He has made,* and that *He has mercy on all,* yet the general practice inculcated in the Apocrypha may be summed up in one brief extract from the book of Tobit, which, though it is exceeded by none of the Apocryphal writings in gentleness and sweet tenderness, yet contains the following exhortation: *Pour out thy bread upon the tomb of the righteous, and give not to sinners.* But, indeed, the novelty of Christ's sayings is not the important question. Grant that every one of our Lord's precepts had been uttered before; what then? What does this prove except that the mere utterance of divine precepts was of comparatively little use till quickened by a Spirit? A Plato or a Hillel, or any other that had some glimmering of *the true light that lighteth every man that cometh into the world,* may have anticipated here one, here another, of the sayings of Christ; and, so far as their spirits quickened their words, so far, but no further, did the divine words convey the divine truths. It would be blaspheming God to depreciate the good and great men whom He has created; but in comparison with Christ their teaching was but the baptism of water compared with the baptism of fire. The words might be the same, but the Power behind the words was different; there is no other way of expressing it: philosophers lectured, Christ *lived;* they spoke of love, He was Love; they gave their pupils their words, He gave His pupils His life.

It has been said, even of ordinary men, that

The greatest gift a hero leaves his race
Is to have been a hero.

And this, in all reverence, we may apply to Christ. It was not what He *said*, but what He *was*, that influenced men. The idea of an all-embracing love, including Barbarians as well as Greeks, Gentiles as well as Jews, may possibly have entered the mind of a heathen philosopher or Jewish rabbi (and, indeed, something like it is apparent in the book of Isaiah), may have been communicated to esoteric pupils and discussed in lecture rooms. But something more is required for the salvation of humanity than a philosophic idea. In the words of a modern writer, *Ideas are often poor ghosts; our sun-filled eyes cannot discern them; they pass athwart us in thin vapour and cannot make themselves felt. But sometimes they are made flesh, they breathe upon us with warm breath; they touch us with soft responsive hands; they look upon us with sad sincere eyes, and speak to us in appealing tones. They are clothed in a living soul with all its conflicts, its faith and its love. Then their presence is a power.* And Christ's presence was a Power, a Power that saved men from their sins by imbuing them with His personality. Through the contact of His Spirit the ambitious felt themselves capable of humility, the dishonest of honesty, the impure of purity. His presence was the Word of God inaugurating the Second Creation, the new and spiritual world. It said, "Let there be Righteousness," and there was Righteousness.

Such was the Power that quickened a knot of Galilean fishermen into the Church of Christ;

such was the Power that, through eighteen centuries, has been the source of all good to Christendom—a Power working sometimes through the instrumentality of Priesthoods and Church organizations, and sacred Scriptures, but sometimes, on the other hand, working in spite of these things—in spite of superstitious sacerdotalism, in spite of dry formal dogmatism or lifeless systems of ecclesiastical government, in spite of the idolatrous worship of the letter of the Bible; and, in either case, whether working through these instruments, or in spite of these obstacles, always a Power, a spiritual Power, distinct from systems, dogmas, codes, and books. Let us briefly, it needs must be very briefly, trace the development of the operations of this Power from its first manifestation; and let us conclude by asking ourselves, "To what course of action does this Power lead us Christians now in modern times?"

Place yourselves in imagination among our Lord's Apostles at the time when He was soon to appear no longer among them. What then was to be the fate of those who depended entirely upon His presence? This question was anticipated and answered by Jesus even before His death, and the answer is expressed in the Lord's Supper. It is recorded of an ancient lawgiver that he pledged his countrymen to a perpetual observance of his laws by his perpetual absence. Our Lawgiver, on the other hand, who left us no law but Himself, promised us His perpetual presence. He had

G

previously declared that, wherever two or three of His disciples were gathered together in His Name, He would be present in the midst of them; and had added, that He would be with His disciples always, even till the end of the world. And now, accordingly, as a pledge of the fulfilment of this, on the evening before His death, when He was celebrating as it were His funeral feast, desiring to leave some legacy to His helpless disciples, and having nothing but Himself to leave them, solemnly, by His last will and testament, He bequeathed to them Himself for ever.

The fleshly presence of a friend is often like the scaffolding round a house; it hides that very friendship which it is helping to build. So was it with those earliest disciples who had seen Jesus in the flesh. Before the death of Jesus they had not understood Him; now they were one with Him; before, they were constantly disputing about supremacy, now they were in perfect unity: before, they were continually thinking about themselves, now all thought of self was lost in the thought of Him; before, they were alarmed at the mere prospect of persecution, now they feared nothing. Thus did our Redeemer fulfil His promise to His disciples and manifest His presence in their hearts. Nor did this influence confine itself merely to those who had seen Jesus in the flesh. The Spirit of Christ extended itself to others also, sometimes through the medium of the imposition of hands, sometimes without that medium; but in all recorded cases, through the personal presence of those who had already received the Spirit. And thus from Christian to Christian, through eighteen hundred years, the Christian spirit has been transmitted till it has reached us in these latest days; and we believe that, having Christ's presence in our hearts, we need not desire a law, not even a Christian law, for we are not under a law but under Christ.

And has not Christ been, and is He not still, speaking to us His disciples? Year by year, and day by day, does He not turn for us the pages of the book of history and the book of our own life, that we may read, mark, and inwardly digest His modern word, and by patient study may discern His will and understand the new duties He sets before us? I appeal to you, my brethren, whether in your private lives you might not, if you would, hear the voice of Christ speaking to many of you at this moment in many varied tones of encouragement or warning—through the loss of friends, the failure of health, the disappointment of high expectations, the indefined sense of disquiet, the ruin or demoralization of some of those whom it was in our power to lead to nobler ends, saying perhaps to one of us, *Come unto me, oh, thou that art weary and heavy-laden;* to another, *Thou canst not serve God and mammon;* to another, *It were better for thee that a mill-stone were hung about thy neck and thou wert cast into the depths of the sea, than that thou shouldest cause one of these little ones to stumble:* and to some of us, *Simon, Simon, behold*

Satan hath desired to have thee that he may sift thee as wheat: but I have prayed for thee that thy faith fail not, and when thou art converted, strengthen thy brethren.

But such private utterances as these are easily audible, they are directly inculcated upon us by the constant reading of the New Testament; and the conscience brings them home to our hearts without much need of thought, deliberation, and judgment. It is not these utterances that I wish now to speak of. There are other duties, duties dictated by Christ's spirit, yet not mentioned in the Bible; and there is need of faith and judgment to hear and interpret rightly these promptings of the Spirit. Take for instance Christ's modern teaching on the duty of almsgiving. When we find by experience, or are told on adequate authority, that indiscriminate charity encourages idleness and imposture while it discourages honest industry, that it propagates the plague of pauperism even to the third and fourth generation, and that it degrades and demoralizes the whole nation, then does not Christ through such facts as these distinctly say to us, "Give *not* to everyone that asketh of thee"? Or again take another duty, which is not so much as mentioned in the New Testament—I mean the duty of educating the young. No doubt there have been exaggerated statements made on this subject by some who consider that the universal education of the young would be a panacea for evil. Still, the ignorant brutality of many crimes which force themselves on us in our journals, the ignorance of the simplest laws of nature and political economy manifested in a sad variety of injurious results—in fatal accidents, in the generation and propagation of disease, in hopeless poverty, and in unnecessary and ruinous conflicts between employers and employed — these are facts, and, as facts, they are the very words of Christ plainly commanding us to make education compulsory, or, if you prefer the word, inevitable, for all classes of our countrymen.

It may indeed be said that the kingdom of God consists not in reading or writing, but in joy, and peace, and the Holy Spirit. And even so the Pharisees might have said to Jesus of Nazareth that the kingdom of God consisted not in opening the eyes of the blind or the ears of the deaf, but in the worship of Jehovah. But our Master seems to have attached a higher value than the Pharisees did to the blessings of sight and hearing. Now what is reading but a second modern sense of seeing? and what is writing but a second modern faculty of speaking? each almost as necessary in this age as those senses and faculties which nature herself has bestowed upon us. Therefore, if we rightly understand the spirit of Christ, we shall feel that we are following in His footsteps and obeying His voice when we do what we can to make education universal, even though an unhappy complication of circumstances should unnecessarily limit education to merely secular instruction.

It would be tedious to enumerate the many other duties enjoined on us by the Christian spirit, though Jesus Himself, as far as our records go, left them unmentioned. But, various and numerous as they are, these duties all spring from one and the same principle—that of philanthropy; and their variety and their number arise simply from the variety and number of the new means of philanthropic action discovered in modern times. Speaking roughly, we might say that the characteristic difference between ancient and modern philanthropy is that the former aims at curing, while the latter aims at preventing; the former is moral, the latter intellectual as well as moral. Thus, if it was the task of the early Christians to relieve disease, it is ours to use our new knowledge of sanitary laws for the prevention of disease; if it was theirs to assist the poor, it is ours to destroy the causes of pauperism; if it was the privilege of the first disciples in one emotional shock to convert a sinner from darkness to light by the mere mention of the name of Jesus, it is our less startling duty to remove from our poorer brethren the irresistible temptations to crime, taught by sad experience, that the want of food frequently means the want of spiritual as well as bodily strength, and the absence of education means the presence of brutality, and the absence of the physical decencies of life means the presence of moral indecency; and in a word, that man's unpitied misery means Satan's opportunity.

These new duties are difficult and complex. They require as much faith and love as the duties of the first century, and more thought and judgment. We need for their fulfilment all the aid we can obtain ; and surely we gain no slight aid if we can convince ourselves that we are not inventing these duties for ourselves, but Christ Himself is dictating them to us and supplementing His ancient teaching in such words as these: "Blessed are the thoughtful, blessed are the industrious, blessed are the just. Go preach the kingdom of God, educate the young : reconcile class to class, nation to nation : incite the poor to thrift and self-control; stimulate the rich to labour for their country. In My name shall ye mitigate disease; in My name shall ye destroy the external causes of vice; ye shall diffuse health and happiness, ye shall banish war; and lo! I am with you always, even unto the end of the world."

And now one word with regard to the connection between these duties and the work of the clergy—a subject of some interest perhaps even to a general audience, but specially suitable for a congregation of this kind, which probably contains many future clergymen among its members. It may be said that "There is no necessity for the teachers of religion to meddle with secular details such as have been mentioned above. It is their business to lay a broad and sound basis of theology, and to leave to the laity the application of it. The modern division of labour has assigned dogmatic teaching, together with the inculcation of the ten commandments and the duty of relieving the poor, to the pulpit, and all other details of practical philanthropy to the press; and this division works satisfactorily, or, if unsatisfactorily, less unsatisfactorily than any other proposed division. Besides, it would be unseemly to have the clergy discussing doubtful questions from the pulpit, sometimes right, sometimes wrong, but, whether right or wrong, often inferior in their power of dealing with such subjects to many members of their congregation."

But, to begin with the last objection, it must be confessed that the teaching of the clergy does not at present produce such an impression as to make all propositions of change unreasonable. A friend of mine once declared that most sermons were of the nature of "Essays by amateurs on the woes of humanity." And that modern accusation reminds us of a more ancient charge brought against certain religious teachers, who were said not to touch even with their little finger the heavy burdens of mankind. It is possible that we might make mistakes in detail (as Latimer and Jewel made mistakes), but, if we read and thought and used our professional experience, even our mistakes might easily be more instructive and more helpful and far more interesting than our present correctness.

Then, as to division of labour, lay and clerical, perhaps that division is unreasonable. It would surely be absurd in studying any subject, mathematics for instance, to divide the examples or problems from the book-work or theory so completely as to require distinct times and tutors for the two. We should be justified in predicting that both the theory and the practice would suffer from such a separation. The theory would become dull and unmeaning, the practice desultory and unsystematic. Just these have been the results of the undue division between the theory and practice of Christianity. Men know the New Testament by heart; but they do not know how to apply it, or to work in the spirit of it: they have not a sufficient number of examples, modern as well as ancient, to give point and life to it; and hence the New Testament is comparatively unmeaning; their theory of Christianity is lifeless, and their life is comparatively unchristian. Our Lord was not content to tell men to love their neighbours as themselves. He gave His hearers a practical instance of neighbourly conduct. Unless illustrated by similar practical instances adapted to our times, it is to be feared that our "high theology" goes flying over the heads of most of our congregations without producing much perceptible effect upon their week-day life.

But the strongest argument for connecting practical philanthropy with Christianity is to be found in the example of Christ, and in the history of the Christian Church. Christ sent His disciples to preach the Kingdom of God, but He put them also to heal the sick. Thus practical philanthropy was the sign of the Church ordained by Christ Himself. With this sign the Church has conquered; without it, failed. The sign has assumed different forms in different ages, but, beneath outward differences, it has always been the same, always the most intelligible evidence of the truth of Christianity that could be presented to men; and the Church has never spread more rapidly than when the world has said, *See how these Christians love one another*.

In the earliest ages, the sign of the Church was a startling power of working instantaneous cures. When that gradually passed away it was replaced by systematic congregational effort for the relief of disease and poverty. Then the evils of slavery were mitigated, the cruelty encouraged by the public games and feasts of paganism was protested against, diminished, and finally abolished. The Church taught as a theory that all men were equal in the eyes of God, but it also illustrated the theory by practice. It acknowledged no difference between gentle and simple, rich and poor, in the ranks of its ministers; it encouraged the emancipation of slaves, and sanctioned the good deed by the presence of the Bishop and the solemn associations of the house of God. Again, the Church preached peace and good-will, but it also enforced, in times of almost continuous warfare, the truce of God. The Church protested generally against injustice and oppression in high places: but it also in practice mitigated what it could not entirely prevent, by making its roof a sanctuary for the fugitive. In this, as perhaps in other matters, there was evil mixed with the good; there was an occasional taint of ecclesiastical arrogance and priestly ambition. But who that reads history can fail to see that it was by this course of active philanthropy that the Church, guiding, not following the world, commended itself to the hearts of the poor and the conscience of the rich, and thus retained its ascendency over the minds of men even in later times when its faults might seem to have exceeded its virtues.

Now turn from the past to the present, not to the actual but to an ideal present, and imagine an ideal National Church, and an ideal ecclesiastical Council adequately representing the Church, laity as well as clergy, and concentrating within itself the Christian action of the whole people. And let us conclude by considering the nature of the tasks to which our ideal Council would most earnestly devote themselves.

Some of their time might possibly be spent in arraigning pestilent heretics and condemning irreligious publications; but it would also be the privilege and duty of such a Council to provide for the publication of a purer literature, and for making the Bible more intelligible to the poorer classes. Some time might be devoted to the minutiæ of vestments, ceremonies, and services of the Church; but some time also to the consideration of measures for the improvement of the social condition of the masses of the people. It might occasionally be a necessary though a painful task to justify by argument the existence of an Established and Endowed Church; but it would be a more welcome and frequent duty to ponder the wants of all classes of the people, Nonconformists as well as Churchmen, and anxiously to consider the best means for including the whole nation within the National Church.

It would be the business of such an assembly to protest, and to ask the aid of all the leaders of popular opinion in protesting, against any conventional lowering of the standard of Christian morality, against the prevalence of any popular amusement that had insensibly become a mere encouragement to vice; against wide-spread dishonesty in evading the payment of taxes, or in employing false weights and measures; against a misconception and disregard of the duties of political life. At the same time such a Council would be a centre regulating and methodizing the action of those countless charitable institutions which at present, by their want of co-operation, leave much good undone, and do some evil. Wielding at its absolute command the powerful engine of the philanthropy of the united nation, such a Council might prove capable of some great and well-directed effort sufficient to extinguish pauperism by emigration, if by no other means. By such a Council it could not have been left to the munificence of a single stranger to take the lead in building roomy and healthy houses for the poor. Such a Council could not have suffered to devolve on one Prelate the burden of planning and executing a gigantic scheme of church extension too vast for a single life. Had such a Council existed, it would not have been left to one statesman to encourage industry and prudence among the working classes by establishing an effectual machinery for guaranteeing their savings, or to another to declare in years gone by, unsupported by any large section of the nation, that children uneducated cannot be expected to become law-obeying citizens. In such a Council as this would have been uttered the first condemnation of slavery in the British colonies, the first protest against the subjection of children to excessive or unduly protracted labour in our manufactories or in our fields. In a word, such a Council would represent the conscience of the country, and, though it might err in its choice of means, and make mistakes in matters of detail, it would always command the interest and regard of the people. It is not enough to say that our Church, if thus represented, would be once more the poor man's Church—it would be the Church of all classes, it would be the Church of *England*. It is not enough to say that our Church would then have no cause to fear disestablishment or disendowment. It would be established in the national heart and endowed with the national affection. Nay, more yet—for even this is little; nor could a nation of proselytes compensate for the deliberate sacrifice of one particle of truth—it would be the best possible representative of Him, who, while He lived on earth, went about doing good and healing all that were oppressed with the Devil, and, when He sent forth His disciples to preach the Kingdom of God, sent them also to heal the sick.

CHRISTIAN PRAYER.

The effectual fervent prayer of a righteous man availeth much.—
ST. JAMES v. 16.

"To labour and to pray" may be called the whole duty of a Christian man. Last Sunday we considered Christian labour: let us to-day consider Christian prayer—its limits and its results. I say its limits, for we are all conscious that we do not pray for all desirable objects. Some seem too trifling and easy of attainment, some too particular and special, some too vast and difficult. Naturally, therefore, there arises the question, where ought we to draw the line between the fit and the unfit objects of prayer?

Such a line has been drawn with great distinctness by many modern teachers. They tell us that we may pray for spiritual blessings, but not for material advantages, except so far as the attainment of the latter evidently depends upon the spiritual quickening of our will. This distinction they justify by declaring that the benefit of prayer consists entirely in the spiritual effect produced upon the person praying. Such, they say, is the only conceivable benefit, for the material world is governed by law, and it is inconceivable that prayer, however *fervent*, should interfere with the laws of nature.

If this be so, it is evident that some of our customary prayers are very circuitously expressed. For, when we pray that God would be pleased *to preserve the kindly fruits of the earth* for us, we mean, on this hypothesis, rather that God would dispose us to preserve them for ourselves by our industry and sagacity. Again, the prayer for fair weather is, on this hypothesis, unmeaning. And above all, it would appear that prayer for friends, which has been described as *binding together the whole round world in golden chains about the feet of God,* is in reality neither more nor less than praying for ourselves. This last conclusion must be a very painful one to all those who have felt prayer for friends to be a reality and not a circuitous method of spiritual self-insurance. Let us therefore investigate the reasons for this conclusion, and, as the reason most commonly alleged is the incompatibility between prayer and law, let us begin by asking ourselves, What do we mean by a "law of nature?"

A law of nature is an assertion that, as far as experience goes, certain facts always have followed certain other facts, and that our experience is so great as to justify us in inferring that the sequence will always continue. To the facts that have invariably preceded we give the name of causes: to those that have invariably followed we give the name of effects. We sometimes talk loosely, as though one set of facts explained or created another. Finding also that this invariable sequence is apparently, in many cases, not to be disturbed by human efforts, and that, in such cases, when it comes into collision with human will, it constrains obedience, we give to this sequence the name of Necessity. The name is but a name. It merely represents a personification of the unpleasing side of invariability. Nor can we strictly say that causes produce or explain effects. What we call the causes teach us when to expect and how to bring about what we call the effects; but there is no creation nor explanation. A stone unsupported in the air falls to the ground: explain that. Why does it fall? It may be replied, that its fall is explained by the law of gravitation, which asserts that every particle of matter attracts every other particle. But what is this law of gravitation except a reassertion of the original fact, viz., that the stone moves to the earth, including besides an assertion of many other similar facts, which have led us to leap beyond our facts to a general assertion of invariability? For all purposes of explaining the stone's fall, to talk about the law of gravitation is as useless as it would be to try to explain the death of a man by saying that all animate beings are mortal. We cannot fully explain, in the strictest sense of the word, any part of any process in the universe. All that we can do is, when we find an unusually vast gap between effect and cause, to fill up the gap by bringing to light unnoticed links of phenomena, themselves both effects and causes; thus we complete the chain to our satisfaction by assimilating the sequence of cause and effect to those ordinary sequences of nature which we call natural, because we are accustomed to them. And when we have done all we can, we can say no more than this, that the sequence now resembles our ordinary experience of sequences. But as for the ultimate cause or creating source of any action, that gap has never yet been filled up, nor has any explanation been given of it. The sceptic must fall back upon the unknown and unknowable; the Atheist must say, " It is, because it is;" the Theist, " It is, because God wills." Upon the will of God, then, we must say, if we believe in a God, depends every part of every invariable process in the universe.

Since therefore God's will is the ultimate cause of all motion in the material world, we can only affect that motion by co-operating with His will. By our bodily actions we continually thus co-operate with God. And is it *a priori* absurd to suppose that God may have also ordained that our wills should under certain circumstances so co-operate with His will as to affect the regulation of the material world? We are not asked to believe that by our wills, expressed in prayers, we can reverse or change all the laws of nature and make the universe work at random, but that it is part of the laws of nature, the higher laws of nature, that our prayers should sometimes, like our actions, influence the material world by co-operating with God. Thus, we are not told to pray against God's laws but according to God's laws, and then we are asked to believe that the prayers of our spirits in accordance with God's laws may be as effectual as the actions of our bodies.

It may seem difficult to explain, or even to conceive how our wills can thus co-operate with God; but it is also even now difficult, if not impossible, to explain how our actions co-operate with God; and before the creation of mankind it might have seemed difficult even to conceive the possibility of such co-operation. If, before the world was tenanted with human beings, a bodiless spirit had been suffered to roam over the surface of the earth, to such a being it might well have seemed impossible that the material substances around it could ever be influenced by spiritual beings like itself. In the first place, there seems so vast a gulf between things spiritual and things material, that it must have been hard to conceive how either can influence the other. And in the second place, the omnipotence and prescience of God might well have seemed to exclude all possibility of co-operation. To imagine that the Creator would allow the face of the earth which

He had created and declared very good to be changed at the will of His own creatures, might well have seemed a mere arrogant dream.

If, therefore, to such a spirit it had been predicted that other spirits would soon be created by God, and that they would strangely alter the form of the visible earth, here penetrating deep beneath the surface, there raising vast piles above the surface; here destroying thick forests, there changing deserts into gardens; here sending rivers to run in fertilizing rillets among the meadows, there driving back and penning up with infrangible barriers the obtrusive ocean—such predictions might well have been rejected as the proud and baseless dream of some rebellious angel. And yet all this and more than all this has been accomplished by human spirits through the instrumentality of human bodies, and we are so accustomed to it that we call it natural.

Now if what might, before experience, have seemed impossible—that the spirits of men can influence the material world—has been proved possible in one way, namely, through the medium of the body, surely we ought to hesitate before affirming that influence exerted by spirit upon matter, without the medium of the body, is impossible and inconceivable. It may be that the hypothesis of such an influence is false, but it certainly is not inconceivable, and we have no right to declare it false till we have examined all evidence that can be adduced in its favour.

Whence shall we obtain evidence? From experiment or from history?

Experiment is here evidently out of the question. Experiment implies doubt, and doubt weakens the force of prayer as naturally as doubt weakens the power of physical action and far more effectually. *Let a man ask in faith*, says St. James, *nothing wavering. For he that wavereth is like a wave of the sea. Let not that man think that he shall receive anything from the Lord.* An availing prayer must come from the very heart of the utterer, wrung by a sense of right and need; the suppliant must feel that in some way, and that the best way, God will answer his prayer. Again, experiment in prayer implies a complete knowledge of our own motives in praying. No reasonable sceptic, endeavouring to confute our belief in prayer, would require of us to prove that a selfish or ambitious or half-hearted prayer obtains fulfilment. But it is difficult to gauge our motives and feelings, difficult to determine how far we were praying selfishly, how far unselfishly, hard again to say how far external circumstances may have been modified in answer to prayer. These considerations seem to shew that we shall not find all the evidence we require (we may find some) in our several experiences of the results of prayer, and that an experimental prayer is a contradiction in terms.

If our own experience gives us but insufficient help, still less is the help afforded by the experience of others as recorded in history. For there we find countless instances of seemingly unanswered prayer. Wherever a ship has gone down at sea with some brief notice of its peril, there have been prayers enough and earnest enough, that the winds might be stilled, the waves calmed; and of these prayers how many have been apparently answered? Wherever, in past ages, the approaching roar of battle round a city's walls has warned the weak and helpless, who can only pray, that now, if ever, prayer is needful—there have gone up, we needs must think there *have* gone up to the very ear of God, prayers from mothers and children for husbands, fathers, and brothers, prayers for country, for life, and for honour; and of these prayers how many have been apparently answered? There may be, there are on record, some instances where the tempest has suddenly ceased, or where a hostile multitude has been beaten from its prey by some sudden intervention of nature, by unexpected relief of human aid, by preternatural valour, or by some other event so unforeseen and seasonable as to appear God's very answer to His suppliants. But, against the few instances of prayer thus answered, it may be alleged that they are so rare that they count as nothing in the face of the innumerable instances of prayer seemingly unanswered. They are like the votive tablets offered by shipwrecked mariners in gratitude for their preservation, to which appeal was made by the priest as tokens of God's preserving care; whereupon the Atheist replied, "But where are the votive tablets of those who were not preserved?" On the whole, it cannot be denied that, from the mere testimony of history, there would appear to be a great waste of genuine prayer.

But history reveals a waste of action, as well as waste of prayer, and yet we act; and many of us believe that the waste is only in appearance. Again, nature reveals waste; and it has become trite to say that out of a hundred seeds some one or two fulfil their seeming object, and the rest, as far as man can see, perish objectless. Yet many of us believe, partly from the testimony of the intuitions of our hearts, partly from other evidence derived from nature, partly from the revelations of God's nature contained in the Bible, that God is a God of order, that every apparently wasted seed is wafted on its apparently objectless errand by an invisible angel of God, and that there is no such thing as waste in nature. As therefore some of us believe, in spite of the evidence of our eye-sight, that there is no waste in nature and no waste in action, may we not as reasonably believe, in spite of the same evidence, that there is no waste in prayer?

It may be replied "You may so believe, if you can obtain the same evidence as convinces us that action in many cases effects its object and in all cases effects something. But, at present, you have only proved a negative, that to believe in the power of prayer is not *a priori* unreasonable.

This we admit. We now want positive evidence to prove that your belief is reasonable."

Whence are we to procure this positive testimony? We have shown that we cannot employ experiment: we have appealed to history in vain. We have nothing — nothing but faith and hope and the distinct experience and statements of Christ. Yet I think, even if we were not Christians, if we were but believers in a noble Theism, we might count faith and hope for something. If God made men and God is good, then one would suppose that the aspirations He has allowed to spring up in His highest creatures, with a vigour proportioned to their moral and intellectual development, are not likely to be altogether false or purposeless; and among the higher races of mankind, it has been a belief, so universal as to be sometimes called an intuition, that Nature, or the Ruler of nature sympathizes with humanity. There are indeed races so undeveloped as to have not so much as a name for God in their language; there are others to whom God is the greatest evil; among these there can be no belief in the sympathy of Nature. But among the leading nations of the world there has always been a faith echoing the sublime utterance of the Hebrew Poet: *At his word the stormy wind ariseth which lifteth up the waves thereof. They are carried up to the heaven and down again to the deep. So when they cry unto the Lord in their trouble, he delivereth them out of their distress.* Sceptics may withhold their belief on the ground that this sympathy of Nature is but a subject of hope, not a demonstrated fact. That attitude of neutrality is intelligible. Others may go further and may boldly assert with Pliny that it is ludicrous to suppose that the Highest, whatever it be, takes care for human things; but then they ought also, in consistency, to go further still with him, in declaring that man is the most wretched of creatures (since no other has wants transcending the bounds of its nature) and that humanity is a lie uniting the greatest poverty with the greatest pride. This has at least the merit of consistency. If we deny that God is love, or deny that God made mankind, then we can with logical impunity deny also that there is any truth in human aspirations, and any intended satisfaction for human cravings; but if we shrink from the former denial we must shrink from the latter also.

Further, this intuition or belief not only exists but exerts a beneficial effect in developing our nature. For, surely it must be helpful for erring mortals if, while wandering through the dusky maze of this dim life, they can discern something of the vision of Milton, and can be inspired by it with something of his belief:—

> *O welcome pure-eyed Faith, white-handed Hope,*
> *Thou hovering angel girt with golden wings,*
> *I see ye visibly and now believe*
> *That He, the supreme Good, to whom all things ill*
> *Are but as slavish offices of vengeance*
> *Would send a glistening guardian, if need were,*
> *To keep my life and honour unassailed.*

Surely such a Creed might inspire the wish that it might be true even in those to whom God is no more than the Unknown and Unknowable. Even Atheists might wish they could believe in a God of goodness, and might admit that such a belief, if sincerely held, would tend more to the happiness and the development and the ennobling of mankind than mere self-dependence. But if we, who are not Atheists, admit this, we must admit more. For, acknowledging a God of goodness, we are bound also to acknowledge that in every belief that makes men happier and nobler, and therefore in this belief, there must be some elements, at least, of truth and goodness.

Thus it appears that, even though, without believing in Christ, we acknowledged a divine goodness ruling the world, we might derive hence some support for our faith in a sympathizing Providence. But being more than Theists, being Christians, we shall find our most convincing evidence in the life of Christ. I know indeed that it is customary to assert that many of our Lord's recorded sayings on the subject of prayer were invented or modified by His disciples. But what disciples were likely to invent so hard a saying as this for instance, *I say unto you that if two of you shall agree on earth as touching anything that they shall ask, it shall be done for them of My Father which is in Heaven?* Again, if there are any reputed words of Christ, of which we can be sure that they are really His, they are the words of the Lord's Prayer. And therefore we have the best possible evidence for believing that our Lord Himself, while He taught us to say *Thy will be done*, taught us also to say, *Give us this day our daily bread*. But these passages are sufficient (and there are many others) to show that our Lord did not recognize the distinction of prayer against which we are contending. Yet, so far from declaring that all things are possible in the sense of all things being attainable by prayer, on one occasion at least He taught or left us to infer the contrary. For in one of the most solemn of all His recorded utterances He said in prayer to the Father, *If it be possible let this cup pass from me*—and we know it was not possible. Placing these words by the side of those quoted above, which appear to say that all things are possible to prayer, we may gather what Christ's teaching really was. It was not that the will of God was liable to be changed by much speaking of men, but that prayer was an appointed means, like action, for recognising and co-operating with the divine Providence. The Spirit of God, Christ taught us, would inspire every assembly of His disciples so that, in the act of expressing to Him their heart's desires, they should recognise the will of God and conform their desires to His; thus, praying according to the Father's will, they would obtain their own desires. If it be asked, by way of objection, " Why pray at all ? since, whether we pray or not, everything will occur in the way prescribed by God's pleasure and in no other way,"—the answer is obvious, "Why act at all? since, whether we act or not, everything will occur according to God's pleasure and in no other way." Just as our experience of nature teaches us to act for certain objects for which we are bound to strive, though, it may be, God has not intended us, in this or that particular instance to obtain our desire, so we are taught by our spiritual nature and by Christ, our spiritual teacher, to pray for many things that we may perhaps not obtain, for all things that may seem to us demanded by the necessities of our physical, mental, and moral welfare,—in a word for everything that may seem to us the *daily bread* of life. And we are to pray thus in the belief that by our prayers we shall either obtain our desires, or finding our desires inconsistent with God's will, we shall desire no longer.

Our conclusion is that prayer is the expression of the desires of the heart to God, as to a Father; that whatever may be lawfully desired in His presence may be lawfully prayed for; that by prayer we may conceivably co-operate with God as we co-operate with Him by action; lastly, that the efficacy of prayer can never be demonstrated by experiment nor by tabulated results, but that the proof of it must in the main depend upon our faith in the aspirations of the higher races of mankind and in the teaching and practice of Christ. The evidence derivable from Christ's life is so full and direct that we need not further dwell on it.

But it may be worth while, before concluding, to point out rather more in detail the importance of prayer to Christians when it is freed from unnatural limitations, and its power to develop in us faith and obedience toward God and love toward our neighbour. It may be well that we should also attempt to realise how much prayer has done for us, and how great a blank would be left in our lives if prayer were taken away.

It is easy for a satirist to laugh to scorn the errors of mis-directed prayer and to include in one condemnation the conqueror's prayer for empire, the child's prayer for fair weather, and the widow's prayer for her only son at sea. But is it not better for us that we should take our real desires day by day and lay them at the feet of God and straighten them by the rule of His will, daily detecting and amending their crookedness, than that we should lead as it were two divided existences, praying without life and living without prayer?

You have been in the habit, many of you, I trust, of thus laying your most earnest wishes at the throne of the Father, and I ask you whether you have not derived even from the prayers that you now consider ill-judged, much spiritual help and much knowledge of God's will. Look back upon the prayers of your youth and your childhood. They may be very different from the prayers that you would frame now, or will frame in still more mature age; but you have no cause to be ashamed or to repent of them. Is it not true that you learned God's will by confessing your will to Him in the form of prayer? Does not your experience teach you that you never gained anything from an insincere prayer however submissively orthodox, but you frequently gained much from very foolish prayers, that represented your real heart's desire? Is it not true that some of your prayers, which at first seemed right and natural, gradually, in the solemn silence of God's presence-chamber, were made, you know not how, to jar upon the conscience, and to seem querulous or trifling, unworthy of the Father's ear? On the other hand some of your early prayers for temporal blessings are perhaps still retained unaltered. And have they not greatly influenced your life? Have they not cleansed for you labours and joys, friendships and social relations, that the prayerless world called common? Have they not each day stimulated you to new effort, each night comforted you after new failure? Have they not, as months and years rolled on, perceptibly modified your character and been to you as it were—

The hands
That reach through darkness moulding men.

Lastly have they not, in some cases, already met with strange and almost marvellous fulfilments that have strengthened your faith and trust in a God who answers prayer?

Now, on the other hand, imagine, if you can, a universal practice established limiting prayer to spiritual blessings for oneself, or rather (if our reformers are to be logically consistent) not limiting prayer at all, but (since there are laws of spiritual as well as of material nature) destroying prayer and substituting for it meditation on God's nature and the relations between God and man. What would have been the influence of such a practice upon your lives? We have all of us, I suppose, been taught from a very early age to pray not only for ourselves that God would make us good but also that He would be pleased to bless our friends. Thus prayer, from our earliest childhood, is connected with the dearest and most familiar names and derives from them much of its life and power. Even now, though childhood be long past, you must feel sometimes that such names as these have influence on your prayer. They can sometimes recall the wandering thoughts and fix the unsteady mind when the most sacred names and solemn phrases pass unmeaningly from your lips. The very highest ideal that a little child can have of God, is, the Being to whom he prays for his father or mother; and many a man in the life-long attempt to lift himself up in heart and soul to that vague, distant God whom no man hath seen nor can see, has been raised, as upon celestial wings, by the daily repeated prayers for friends, whose faces are the dear realities of his life. But if, even now, when Christ should be a sufficient help to prayer, the names of friends are helpful, how would it have been with us during childhood, when God and Christ were but far-off mysteries to us, if we had not been allowed to pray for friends? Would not the act of praying have been little but an empty form?

And are we to believe that all this training, divine at least in its results, was the mere error of self-conceit, that it ought logically to be discontinued, and that if any benefit at all was ever derived from the delusion, it was because, while the child fancied he was praying for his parents and friends, he was really praying for himself? We are frequently reproached, and not altogether without reason, for the spiritual selfishness said to be inherent in religious people: is it then a likely cure for religious selfishness to make self-love instead of love of others the fountain-head of prayer, to sever us, as soon as we enter into communion with God the Father, from the communion of men our brethren, to make us say "My Father" where Christ taught us to say "Our Father," and, while we are encouraged to work for the benefit of others, to discourage us from praying for anybody but ourselves? If it be so, surely there is no proportion between the two parts of Christian duty, and the less of prayer and the more of work the better.

* The subject of praying for friends is closely connected with one of the deepest questions of

---

* The passage beginning here and ending on the top of page 117 was not read when this sermon was preached.

spiritual life, which must not be entirely omitted. Insensibly we appear to have been led to something like a law of prayer. We may pray for everything that we feel to be part of the "daily bread" of our spiritual, mental, and physical life. Now we are in the habit of praying daily for our living friends. What when they die? Must those dear names which once gave prayer all its meaning and for so many years have never once been omitted by day or night, be omitted now? And if a dire necessity is to enforce their omission, can death be said to have lost its sting, and the grave be declared to have gained no victory? The day of loss is bitter, but how much more bitter the night when we kneel down and find that death has robbed us both of our friend and of our prayer! Our heart's wish remains the same, the dear familiar words rise instinctively to our lips, but death comes between our Father and us, and laying his cold hand upon our lips forbids the utterance. Is it possible that death should have such power?

On a subject of such importance I prefer, before giving my private opinion, to quote from a treatise on the Articles of the Church of England, composed by the Bishop of this Diocese, and much used in this University. After observing that the practice of praying for the dead " dates unquestionably from the second century " the author continues thus. " It has been so common to admit the false premiss of the Romanist divines (viz. that prayer for the dead presupposes a purgatory) that it is to many minds difficult to understand on what principles the early Christians used such prayers. One of these principles was doubtless that all things unknown are to us future. Present and future are but relative ideas. To God nothing is future, all things are present. But to man that is future of which he is ignorant." From this explanation I infer that, since we are ignorant of the state after death of any particular person, it may be regarded as future by us for the purposes of prayer. No certain instance of prayer for the dead can be found in the New Testament, but few critics will deny that there is a very strong probability that Onesiphorus was dead at the time when St. Paul uttered the prayer, "May the Lord grant mercy to him." This view is also adopted in Dean Alford's Commentary.

My own feeling is that, in the matter of prayer, Christian precedent, even though it date "unquestionably from the second century," cannot be all-powerful, although it should have its weight. We cannot honestly pray for that about which we have ceased to entertain hope, even though our fellow-Christian prayed for it sixteen hundred years ago. If the language, necessarily metaphorical, describing the states of æonian life and æonian chastisement awaiting human souls after death, appears to you to preclude all possibility of further development and purification, and therefore to leave no room for hope and wish, then I do not see what room there is for prayer, which is merely a wish in words.

Although the past may be unknown to us, and the discovery of what has taken place in the unknown past may be to us an unknown future, yet the fixedness of the past must needs prevent that kind of wish and hope about it which is essential to prayer. Not even a child would ask his father to undo the unknown deed of yesterday.

But if you believe that we know little or nothing about the future state of human souls; if you believe that there may be many future states in which a soul may rise from grade to grade in unending development, in the process of conformation to God's Image, then prayer for the dead becomes reasonable and natural. And certainly the intense wish to pray for the dead, is, in itself, to some extent a justification of prayer. I do not for a moment maintain that such prayers have not been superstitiously degraded, or that the Reformers were not justified in discountenancing the practice of public prayer for the dead, finding it, as they found it, so perverted and corrupted; but I cannot think that they would have desired for ever to deny to Christians the comfort of private prayer for their departed friends. Indeed, if you ought not to pray, ought you to wish?

Can it be unlawful to express a wish, and yet lawful to cherish a wish as long as it is unexpressed —and that in the presence of an all-knowing Father? Surely not. Therefore the alternative appears to be that either we are bound to eradicate all wishes for the welfare of the dead, or retaining the wish we may express the wish in prayer. I do not feel justified in dictating to you which of these two courses you should adopt. It must depend upon your faith in God, and your faith in the rightfulness of your wishes for the dead. But if you believe such wishes as these come from God, if you can look on sin and death, and yet believe that God is the Father of all, if you can see " beneath the abyss of hell a bottomless abyss of love," then I think you need not deny yourselves in private that most consoling communion with God, which soothes the bitter pain of death-bed parting, and brings the saints above into close fellowship with Christ's soldiers militant on earth, deepening the divine impressions wrought daily by the dead upon the living, giving to each of us an invisible circle of unchanging faces that watch our course on earth, and conferring new strength and sanction on the sacred bond of the family, by raising it above the grasp of death.

Let me but add that those to whom prayer for the dead may seem strange and scarcely right, may sometimes find some legitimate strength in such mention of the dead as is found in our Prayer for the Church Militant. Whatever may be our belief about the future states of human souls, it must be lawful to all, while mentioning the familiar name in the familiar place, to *bless God's Holy Name for His servants departed this life in His faith and fear, beseeching Him to give us grace so to follow their good examples, that with them we may be partakers of His heavenly kingdom.*

Such and so vast is or might be the influence of faithful prayer. Yet still there is, perhaps, an uneasy feeling in many of us that we ought not to pray for many things for which men prayed in ancient times; and this is true, but a truth not difficult to explain. In the first place, many desires natural to humanity can in modern times be easily satisfied by the results of modern science. Now, where a desire can easily be satisfied by action, there is not felt the need of prayer. To take an illustration, a mother who saw her child apparently dying, might, if no remedy were at hand, resort to prayer; but if medical science had discovered a certain remedy, prayer would give place to action combined with praise. And this is but a type of a large class of similar cases where prayer once would have been natural, but now would be unnatural. In the second place, there can be no doubt that our increased knowledge of what we call the laws of nature does, and ought to, greatly diminish the number of objects for which we pray. But, if we cease to pray, it ought to be, not because our desires seem contrary to necessity, but because they seem unreasonable and contrary to God's will. There is a great difference between obeying law and will, between making a surrender to necessity and a sacrifice to a Father. If God, by revealing to us new facts of order and harmonious beauty, impresses our mind with the belief that the visible unchanging order represents His will, then, though there is no necessity, for necessity implies the sense of compulsion, yet the revelation has no less power to turn our heart's prayers to silence. But mark the difference between the effect of obeying a necessity and a Father. In the one case we yield the sullen obedience of a slave, in the other, the loving obedience of children. In the one case we are silent, but our desires are as disorderly and as rebellious as ever; in the other case, our prayers are silent, but it is because our desires are self-suppressed. In the former case we can say like rebels to Necessity, "Our wills are ours;" in the latter, like children to a Father, "Our wills are ours to make them Thine."

For these reasons, as we grow up from childhood to manhood and learn from experience more of God's will, our prayers will undergo a change. The child, who has been told that God loves little children, and who infers that He intends children to be happy, may, without harm, pray that the weather may be fair simply for his particular happiness. But the man, who knows from experience and instruction that such weather as may be convenient to him may be injurious to others, and that those invariable sequences which we call the consequences of natural phenomena are very vast and complicated, will, if he be unselfish, feel a certain shame at praying or even wishing for a change of the weather, merely to suit his own interests.

But, on the other hand, suppose a whole people in danger of famine, or at all events, of grievous want, owing to an unusual condition of the weather. Suppose the fields white and ready for the harvest, the husbandman ready for work, and all the nation praising the God who appointed times and seasons, rain and sunshine, sowing and reaping for men; when suddenly and, as it seems to us, unnaturally, there comes continuous rain for days upon days spoiling and destroying the kindly fruits of the earth, while helpless industry looks on in enforced idleness. At such a moment, when God seems to have two wills, with one hand giving, and with the other taking away, then we, in ignorance which may be His will, may rightly express our wills to Him in prayer. And we have the authority of Christ and His Apostles and Prophets for believing that such a prayer sincerely uttered may of itself, in accordance with God's natural laws, so co-operate with God as to modify the working of the material world. I do not say such a prayer may always be lawful. If hereafter God should reveal to us so much more of the sequence of phenomena in His universe, as to make it clear that laws of the same kind as regulate the motions of the planets, regulate also with as little deviation the weather of our earth—then probably we should be silenced by our enlarged knowledge of the stupendous magnitude of the orderly system with which our prayers would interfere. But at present this is not our condition. At present the causes on which the weather depends are not ascertained with astronomical exactitude. On the contrary, it is known that man and man's work influences rain, wind, clouds and climate; and it has been elaborately and graphically shewn how a gardener's spadeful more or less, determining a swallow's life or death, and the extinction or non-extinction of a few hundred insects, may create a blight, a deluge, a devastation, and thus a dry desert in the place of a well-watered land.

Lastly, if the nation prays and the rain still falls, is the prayer wasted? Do not believe it. Let me once more remind you of the prayer of Christ, *Let this cup pass from Me.* The petition was not granted; the cup did not pass from Him. To the eye of the world the prayer was wasted, but to the eye of faith there appeared an answer in the form of an angel from heaven strengthening Him. Doubt not that in like manner every sincere and unselfish prayer that ever goes up to heaven from your lips will summon down from heaven a responsive angel to strengthen you. Only beware lest while you raise yourselves in modern conceit above the infirmities of Christ your Lord, you deprive yourselves of that divine strength which is made perfect in human weakness.

THE SIGNS OF THE CHURCH.

We see not our signs.—PSALM lxxiv. 9.

"WHAT are the signs of a Christian Church?" is a question often asked in former times, and, for many reasons, well worth asking now. The immediate answer to this question has been, happily for us, given by Our Lord Himself: and, in His words, the sign of the Church is not the collection of a body of correct dogmas, not the preservation and observance of a code, not the unbroken series of a divinely ordained priesthood, not the elaboration of solemn rites and tasteful ceremonies, but —*by this shall men know that ye are my disciples, if ye have love one toward another.*

The sign of a Christian Church is, therefore, *love.* But love cannot be called a "sign" until it is manifested in perceptible effects. Properly speaking then, not love but loving action, or, as we should express it in modern language, active philanthropy, is the sign of a Church of Christ. This philanthropic action has assumed different shapes in different ages, but has never been absent from a genuine Christian Church.

In the Apostolic Church these "signs" consisted especially in acts of healing. Christ sent His disciples to preach the kingdom of God, but their preaching was made more effective by the "signs" of healing. Christ proved, or if you prefer to express it so, convinced men that He was the Healer of the soul by showing that He could heal the body. These acts of healing were not arbitrary "signs" or accidental accompaniments, but the natural results of Christian preaching; in many cases occurring without the expressed wish, and even without the knowledge, of the preacher. The message of light and life passing from the Ambassador of Christ to those that lay in darkness and shadow of death, and rolling away the darkness of superstitious terror from the soul, seemed to bring, in natural companionship, physical as well as spiritual health. The effect produced by the proclamation of the Gospel in those early days may be illustrated by a passage in the Acts of the Apostles, which describes how Philip, on entering Samaria, preached the Kingdom of God: *and unclean spirits crying with loud voice came out of many that were possessed; and many that were possessed and many taken with palsies, and that were lame, were healed, and there was great joy in that city.* Thus did Christ and His Apostles connect the spiritual and the material happiness of men. Such were the signs that aided the Gospel to commend itself as

Good News in the Apostolic Church: and with these signs the Church grew and prospered.

In the next age the signs were different, but not absent. The wonderful power of producing instantaneous cures rapidly diminished, and before very long vanished from the Church. But still, in spite of theological differences, the true spirit of Christian love, using as its instrument a systematic Church organization, effected for the relief of the poor and the cure of the sick results that startled their antagonists into admiration, and made the Pagans cry: *See how these Christians love one another!*

It was also in its destructive "signs" that Christianity now manifested itself, not merely organizing almsgiving and reducing practical pity to a Church system, but also destroying the superstitious idolatries that had crushed hope and faith out of men's hearts; destroying the gladiatorial exhibitions that had degraded their victims to the level of wild beasts and the spectators to the level of fiends; and lastly, mitigating, though it could not destroy, the horrors of war. Thus, still in the front of the world, in the van of progress, and, in the strength of her "signs," commending herself to the hearts of men, the Church found entrance into hovels and alleys where philosophy would have lectured to deaf ears; and thus the Church still worked and grew and prospered.

If destructive signs had been characteristic of this age, during the next age it might be said that the Church rather manifested its signs in protecting. Faults and corruptions had crept in: theological discord was rampant. But, when the barbarian beat at the gate of Rome and threatened to set up violence as the dominant principle of the earth, to blot out learning beneath the darkness of ignorance, and to drown the traditions of civilization amid the din of anarchy, it was the Church that put back the mailed hand of the intruding warrior, drawing the weak suppliant to the inviolable sanctuary of the altar; it was the Church that would know no difference between Roman and barbarian, and, recognising a common Father, would recognise all men as brothers. And therefore, in spite of many faults and increasing corruptions, yet still in the front of the world, with the conspicuous sign of the sanctuary, standing up against the strong as the refuge of the weak, the Church still grew and prospered.

As time went on the faults and corruptions of the Church increased; but the signs were still there. There was much in the Church that to poor unlearned men might seem unnecessary and unintelligible; some things that to plain blunt men might seem scarcely right and honest: but still there were some "signs" that could be understood by all alike, even the plainest and poorest. It was, as a rule, the Church that encouraged learning, and that protested against indiscriminate warfare, against oppression and exaction; it was round some Church or monastery that the dwellings of peaceful traders and husbandmen clustered for security, and became the nucleus of great cities; it was the Church that favoured the enfranchisement of serfs, the Church that rebuked violence and profligacy in high places; it was in the Church alone that a poor husbandman or villein could rise to the highest throne in Europe, to wear the papal tiara, dictating conditions and offering crowns to kings and emperors. Therefore, in spite of many faults, and in spite of increasing corruptions, still in the front of the world, leading the way alike in moral and mental culture, the Church still grew and prospered.

But at last the faults began to overpower the signs. The Church began to respect persons and to pay court to wealth, not as the exception, but as the rule. It associated itself with the luxurious, the wealthy, and the powerful; and dissociated itself from the poor and the oppressed. The Church was tempted, as Christ had been tempted, to bow down and worship Satan in order to obtain dominion over the world; and where Christ had resisted, the Church succumbed. It had hoped by doing a little evil, by using a little worldly policy, a little craft, a little force, to do a great good and to obtain a universal empire that should be the means of spiritualizing the world. But the world would not be thus used as a tool by the Church: on the contrary, the Church became the tool of the world. Thus it came to pass that Christ's forgiveness was hawked about the streets for money—so at least it appeared to plain poor men—and the eternal peace of the dying could be secured by a bequest to a monastic order. Thus the Church became no longer the poor men's Church but the rich men's; the Church of knights and kings and emperors, but no longer the Church of serfs and villeins and ploughmen. Endowments poured in thickly; priests abounded; monasteries became numerous and wealthy; churches rose, densely dotting the land; but the signs of the Church were absent or fast vanishing: and, though the body of the Church flourished, its spirit seemed on the point of death.

Then, after many warnings, God sent a spirit of righteous indignation into the hearts of men; and religious liberty, unconsciously fostering political liberty, became a power in the world. Thus once again in England (to confine ourselves to our own country) the Church became the people's Church; and citizens of London flocked to Paul's Cross to hear Latimer preach, and to take part in the national protest against Papal encroachments. Never since then in England, has the English Church been so completely identified with the English people, except for one brief period when the cheers of the crowd resounding from Westminster Hall past Temple Bar carried into the heart of the city the news of the acquittal of those Seven Bishops who have earned for the Church the right to say that on one single occasion she stood forward as the champion of English liberty.

For now, where are our "signs?" Ask the great masses of the English working-classes what they think of the Church of England, and what will be their answer? They will tell you, not that they are hostile to the Church, not that they are the enemies of Christianity; but that "Christianity and Church are to them names of no interest; they are for the rich. To the poor the Gospel brings no good news." By quoting certain Bible texts, you may attempt to prove certain theological dogmas to them; but the dogmas have no life for them; and they do not recognize the Bible as an authority. Again, you may attempt to terrify them with the fear of death, of future judgment, and of everlasting torment: but in these terms they do not believe, nor, if they did believe them, could such a message be a *Gospel*. Lastly, you may attempt more legitimately to preach Christ's Gospel as a Gospel, that is, as a Good News: but this you will find hard. "What," they will ask, "has the Church done for us? What has it done for the poor, the struggling and oppressed, during the last quarter of a century? Was it the Church that extinguished negro slavery? Was it the Church that forwarded or suggested the Factory Acts? Has the Church ever suggested a similar protection for children employed in agriculture? Did the Church help to get us cheap bread by removing the Corn Laws? Did it lend a hand to liberty by aiding political reform five-and-thirty years ago? In the contests between capitalists and labourers, has the Church ever sided but with the rich? Has the Church done anything to help emigration, to give a fair chance to co-operative experiments, or even to encourage economy by suggesting state security for the accumulations of the poor? Religion, it is true, has played an important part in connection with education, and sect has vied with sect in establishing schools for the purpose of propagating denominational doctrines; but what is the connection most familiar to all of us between religion and education? is not religion our great obstacle? Is not religion, in connection with education, best known through the well-known phrase *the religious difficulty?*" * And all this but represents the calmer and more tranquil feelings of the poorer classes: but another phase of feeling, far more bitter and desperate, and, let us hope far more rare, is described in some words that lately appeared in the public journals as the last expression of a despairing suicide. "It is of no use speaking to me about the Bible, for I don't believe in it. Why don't the rich keep to it better, if it is true? No, they do not believe in it, but pay men to preach to the poor, to frighten them from stealing from the rich." *

What are we to say to such terrible accusations as these? I think we ought to say that they are in part true; but that whatever truth may be in them condemns not Christ, but us. We, we are in

---

* It need scarcely be pointed out that I did not intend to adopt this language as representing the absolute truth, but as the opinion current among large sections of the poorer classes, and as containing a good deal of truth.

fault, not our Master. We have narrowed down Christian duty to the performance of a few works specially mentioned in the New Testament: but that is not Christ's fault. Christ did not tell us that we are to do nothing but such good works as are specially mentioned in the Gospels: He did not profess to dictate a complete list of Christian duties; He did not construct for us a code or Christian Law; He bequeathed to us a spirit of love in which the Church is to act free and unshackled, adapting its action to the varying circumstances of each age. In the early Church society was simpler, knowledge less extensive than it is now. The one obvious way of showing one's love for one's fellow-man was in those days, assisting the poor, and healing the sick. Consequently these duties are mentioned over and over again in the pages of the New Testament. But now, society has become far more complex; our knowledge has greatly increased and has taught us much that was then unknown of the causes of poverty and of sickness. We have now learned that alms-giving is a very dangerous means of relieving poverty, that it often does more harm than good, by diminishing self-respect and discouraging thrift and industry; we have learned to prefer means less attractive and picturesque, more indirect and tardy in their operation, means likely rather to affect the future than the present generation, but in the end likely to prove more permanently effective; such means, for example, as the enlargement of fields of labour, whether at home or abroad; the encouragement and inculcation of temperance; the encouragement of self-respect by providing for the poor houses and homes fit for human beings to live in; the encouragement of intellectual tastes by providing sources of legitimate enjoyment and recreation; and lastly the systematic education of the young, which, if rightly conducted, ought to stimulate at once self-respect, intelligence, temperance and industry. These new duties therefore take the place, to a great extent, of the old duty of alms-giving; and they ought to fill the same prominent position in the modern Church as alms-giving once occupied in the early days of Christianity. It would not be difficult to enumerate other modern duties prescribed by modern circumstances. Generally it may be said that, whereas in old times it was the duty of the Christian Church to *cure*, it is now our duty to *prevent*. And these new *preventive* duties are as much enjoined upon us by the Spirit of Christ, and as closely connected with our religious life as though they were specially mentioned in the Sermon on the Mount and in every chapter of every Epistle in the New Testament.

If it should be asserted that Christian life, or at all events Christian teaching, cannot enter into minute details of this kind, I think a reply might be easily found in the writings of St. Paul. That Apostle at all events, in the midst of all his high theology did not scorn details of social life and even of domestic relations. The relations of master and slave, of husband and wife, father and child, subject and ruler, as well as the whole system of Church government and the relations between members of the congregation, are not too petty to be treated of in his Epistles. He begins perhaps by deducing and elaborating some great theological truth as a basis; but almost every Epistle has its superstructure of plain practical duty. And we ought to be no less practical in applying our Christian theology to our Christian duties, not to the duties of the first, but to those of the nineteenth century.

We are far too diffident about the power of the Christian spirit, far too prone to convert our Christian freedom into a Christian law, and to make our religion a series of *Thou shalt nots*. Just as our artistic representations of purity are too often created by taking every trace of human passion out of the human face, so Christianity is not thought perfect till all force and freedom are expelled from it. Yet Christ did not die for men to add to their burdens and to enact a second and more terrible law, but to enable us to lead a free life of natural righteousness. Surely, if Christ were a second time to manifest Himself visibly as a man among us, He would condemn our backwardness. We elaborate our doctrine, we are scrupulous about our ceremonies, we are earnest on points of ecclesiastical government, more than earnest on ecclesiastical vestments. These are our mint, our anise and our cummin. *This ought ye to have done but not to have left the other undone.*

I am speaking of our general tendency, not denying that there are exceptions to it: least of all would I deny that there are patient, self-sacrificing, devout ministers of Christ whose whole lives are devoted to the help of the poor, and to the feeding of the flock committed to them by Christ. But even to some of these I would suggest that wisdom should be combined with their unselfishness, and that too often their life's effort serves but as a kind of insufficient dole, just sufficient to keep beggary and wretchedness alive, without giving them strength enough to rise into self-supporting thrift and godly thankfulness.

We ought to hear the voice of Christ sending out His messengers to preach the Gospel of the nineteenth century, a voice the same yet not the same as of old, different in words, but the same in spirit. *Go, preach the Gospel of God: educate all classes, lighten the pressure of labour; increase the joys and lawful pleasures of life; stir up the rich to labour for their country; lead the poor toward thrift and industry; discourage luxury, and encourage public spirit: Unite together by community of interest employers and employed: where society appears disorganizing itself on the principle of competition, reorganize society on the basis of the Christian congregation. These signs shall follow them that believe. In my name shall they mitigate disease, in my name shall they banish epidemics: they shall diffuse health, happiness and culture: they shall root out the causes of crime, and banish war from the world.*

If it be asked by what means may the Christian Church return to her old position as guide of the world, leading on the way of progress, and conspicuous by her appropriate signs, my answer is, firstly, by a clearer knowledge of Christ, and secondly, by improved organization of Christian philanthropic action. Let us deal with the second point first. I have heard it said, in reference to this point, that the one thing needed is that the clergy should devote less attention to Latin and Greek and more attention to the great questions of the day, to social questions, to history, and, above all, to the history of our own nation. But, whatever truth there may be in this suggestion, it is quite certain that no effectual improvement can be expected till the congregation regularly and systematically co-operates with the clergy. The duties that have been described above are far too varied to allow that even the inculcation and discussion of them, much less the execution, should be appropriated by any one man in a district, or any one class in a kingdom. At present the populous districts of the Metropolis and the larger towns in England are, many of them, in a most pitiful condition. There are exceptions, no doubt, and, as I trust, such exceptions are rapidly on the increase: but, as a rule, the clergyman stands almost alone in his conflict against evil. What we want is, in each district, a Christian army trained to act together for the destruction of evil and the propagation of good in every shape; but what we too often find is a solitary sentinel keeping guard over a half-captured fort, whose sole duty it is from time to time to cry that *all is not well.*

This is not the place, nor is this the time, to enter into the details of the system by which the co-operation of the laity and clergy might be secured and regulated. But one hint, or perhaps one question with its answer may be sufficient to direct your attention to the source whence we must look for reform. What is the reason why the government of the state has for many years commanded, and seems likely for many more years to command, the respect and confidence of the English people? Is it not because the people are duly represented in that government, and because from time to time such changes have been made as have adjusted the government to the changed conditions of the people? Well then, if it cannot be denied that, for more than two hundred and fifty years, there have been no changes made to assimilate our form of Church government with the changing condition of the people, is it to be wondered at that many persons feel that there is something antique and museum-like in the National Church, so that, in some places, they go to violent extremes straining the law in their passion for novelty, while elsewhere they so far hold aloof from the Church and Church affairs that the condition of things may be best described as a clerical autocracy tempered by lay indifference?

But now if all, clergy and laity alike, were to devote themselves to the weightier matters of Christian duty, I mean the improvement of the material, mental and moral condition of their fellow-men through the means suggested to us by modern knowledge, and if they were constantly in the habit of meeting, consulting and co-operating for these purposes, many differences that once seemed vast would sink into insignificance; and all parties in the Church would be more ready to re-echo those noble words of Edward Irving, words that ought to be printed in gold on the door of every theological lecture-room; *There never was any error so false but I could find some truth in it.* Then Church dogmas, and Church ceremonies, and forms of Church government, being brought into continual contact with the golden rule of Christian philanthropy, would by that rule be fairly judged, and estimated at their proper value.

If, turning aside from present painful realities, one might be allowed to imagine a more Christian future, it would not be difficult to picture to ourselves the true ideal of a modern Christian congregation. One can at least imagine a congregation that does not merely meet together once or twice a week on the stated occasions of public worship, but habitually co-operates for other purposes; a congregation in which, while all members have a common object, each member has a different duty; men as well as women taking a part in the congregational work, and even the busiest finding some time for it amid the pressure of private engagements; some visiting the poor, and in such numbers and with such a division of the labour that, while none of the visitors are burdened, the visiting, instead of remaining a series of perfunctory calls, ripens into an intimate and friendly acquaintance between rich and poor; others teaching in the schools; others managing relief-clubs, reading-rooms, libraries; others giving lectures or readings for the instruction or amusement of the poorer members of the congregation—doing, in a word, just what is done now, in the better organized districts, only doing it more effectively because the brain and heart of every member of the congregation would be ready to contribute to the work. And in addition to this we can imagine such a body of Christian workers meeting together, at intervals, not merely for prayer and praise but also for the purpose of comparing their active experiences, giving and receiving advice as to their future efforts. At such meetings it is reasonable to suppose that, besides the improvement and development of the usual methods of philanthropy, new methods would occasionally be suggested. It might be found not impossible for a congregation to make some common effort to improve the houses of the poor in their neighbourhoods, to stimulate elementary education by the establishment of small scholarships for the higher pupils, to establish free libraries, to throw open squares or gardens for the recreation of the poor—there are a thousand shapes in which the congregational energy might usefully embody itself. One can imagine then the Parish Church, a hive of busy workers, the head-quarters of a Christian regiment, the fountain of all the philanthropic action of the neighbourhood, rearing itself in each district as a great "sign" of peace and good-will, proving, as of old, that Christ loves and heals the souls of men, by shewing that He cares for their bodily welfare, and forcing the antagonists of our Religion to repeat the utterance eighteen centuries old: *See how these Christians love one another.* Trust me, such Christian action would be the best possible commentary upon the New Testament, surpassable by no exegetic theology as yet discovered. But we awake from our dream, and lo! it is a dream, and nothing but a dream. Pray earnestly all of you that there may be some one in this assembly so young that he may live to see this dream made a reality.

And now, to come to the second point of reform, the needful increase of the knowledge of Christ. It is quite certain that no amount of dreaming or imagining, or paper systems, or synods, or convocations, can ever make a Church, any more than a parliament can ever make a nation. It is against nature, it is against Christ's method, to begin with the corporate body and afterwards to proceed to the individual. If ever we are to have a genuine Christian Church in England, we must have first a genuine Church spirit working in English men and English women. By a Church spirit I do not mean an ecclesiastical or sectarian spirit: I mean a social spirit, a spirit of Christian companionship or fellowship. What we want therefore is an increase of that faith in Christ and that love of Christ, which shall lift us out of our selfish inertness and antipathies, and make us one with Him, able to feel as He felt, and to love as He loved. Without the spirit of love we can do nothing. It is true that Christian action is essential to Christian love, just as air is necessary to life; but, just as air cannot create life, so no amount of seeming philanthropic action can replace or create Christ's spirit of love.

Well then, we want more love. And one step towards obtaining it, is to know that we are deficient in it. Perhaps some of you are scarcely conscious enough of your deficiency in this respect. You are accustomed, perhaps, in your religious meditations, sometimes to search yourselves whether you are in a state of grace and salvation, and to ask what sign you can obtain of your spiritual condition; but it may not have occurred to you that there is one and only one plain sign mentioned by Christ, which gives an immediate answer to your self-introspective questions. Need I repeat it? *By this shall men know that ye are My disciples, if ye have love one towards another.*

Mark—towards one another, not towards the amiable and interesting, but towards the dull uninteresting and common-place as well, towards those average people whom, may be, your fastidiousness finds it difficult to tolerate. This is the great sign of signs, in which alone you can conquer; and remember, that no spiritual condition is safe unless it has this "sign;" and further—though it ought to be a truism not worth repeating—that no religious dogma, no rite, no ceremony, no worship, is of the slightest importance, except so far as, directly or indirectly, it enables you, or others, to fulfil this, the only Law of Christ's Kingdom, the Law of Love.*

Now, before I turn your hearts toward Christ as the only source whence this divine all-embracing love can be instilled into your hearts, I should like to add one word about the nature of Christian Love. Plain men may think that such a term can need no explanation. Nor ought it: but, unhappily, just as there is a "forensic" righteousness, so also there is a "forensic" love, current in the religious world; and this miserable parody of the divine reality must be cleared away before Christ's genuine Love can take hold of us.

I lay down this rule then, that, before you can love your fellow-creatures, you must see something in them worth loving. Else you will be but a

---

* Most of what follows was omitted when the sermon was preached, for want of time.

hypocrite in saying you love them; and your religion will be a make-believe. You cannot call your fellow-creatures utterly bad, utterly worthless, utterly destitute of all goodness, that is, of all that is worth loving—and yet consistently say you love them. But perhaps you reply, "I love them for Christ's sake, not for their own, nor for anything in them." Well, I appeal to you yourselves, what would you give for the love of a religious person, who came and said to you, "My friend, you are utterly bad, sinful and worthless. I can see nothing to love in you. But I will feed you, and clothe you, and give you alms. This, however, I do, not for your sake, but for Christ's. For Christ has taught me that I ought to love you; and indeed, with Christ's words now rising to my recollection, I think I may venture to add that, though I cannot love anything in you, yet, in a certain sense, and forensically so to speak, I may almost be said to love *you*." Would you not if you had left in you one spark of manly resentment, one breath of God's spirit of honesty and truth--- would you not indignantly cast back such a mere fiction and parody of the divine feeling of love, and infinitely prefer the irreligious and imperfect affection of anyone who could see, or could fancy that he saw something to love in you for your own sake?

Then how are we to love bad people for their own sake? Why, by seeing in them, beneath the badness, something that is good: by seeing, to use the words of Shakespeare *the soul of beauty in things evil*, or, to use the language of the Bible by believing that *God created man in His own image;* and that, however that image may have been defaced or darkened, something of it still remains; nor is there anyone in the world so buried in selfishness, so hardened and polluted by sensuality and vice, but that the eye of Christ could discern in him—even though it might be invisible to all earthly eyes—some lingering vestige of the likeness of God.

But to love bad, and to love common-place people in this honest straightforward way, is the most difficult thing in the world. None of us can see the good in our neighbour's character as we ought to see it; and in proportion as we succeed in seeing it, in that proportion we approximate to Christ who alone sees men as they are. And this leads me back to what was called the second needful point of Christian reform, I mean a clearer knowledge of Christ. For if we could know Christ perfectly, we could love men perfectly. For to know Christ would imply perfect sympathy with Him, identity with Him, and the power to see in men what He saw, and to love men as He loved.

To this then we have come at last, that all depends on knowing Christ more perfectly. And how are we to know Him more perfectly? By fighting against the almost universally prevalent Spirit of Antichrist, which, while admitting His divinity, denies His humanity; by remembering always that He was a Man with the motives and feelings of men; by dwelling not so much on His power, which by His own will was very limited, as on His love, which was illimitable; by throwing ourselves in perfect trust and faith on Him, as being the one Perfect Love, and therefore God; by believing in His divinity, not on the strength of texts here and miracles there (many of which have been assailed, and some of which may be hereafter modified by modern criticism), but on the strength of His whole life and character, as it is clearly and incontrovertibly set forth by the conjoint testimony of the Gospels and of History. Remember also, that you can never have Christ proved or demonstrated to you as an historical fact. Belief in Christ means belief in the infinite power and ultimate supremacy of Love. Then, if you wish to believe this, you must struggle against everything that would shake this belief in your heart; against impurity, against luxury, against indolence, against selfishness in every form, and above all against the fatal spirit of cynicism. Lastly, you must grow in the knowledge and admiration of human goodness; you must be ready to recognise excellence in your own circle of acquaintance, no less than to admire it in the great examples of ancient and modern history; and when you read or hear of the life of a good man, you must accept it as one of the myriad of "broken lights" that bear witness to the one true Light, that lighteth every man that cometh into the world.

Thus growing year by year in the knowledge of goodness, that is, in the knowledge of Christ which passeth knowledge, let us go forward on the path dictated by Christ's Spirit. Each for his own soul is the watchword of Satan: but let us strive to bear one another's burdens. Soldiers of the cross of Christ, let us consider ourselves sent into the world to make war against all evil. And, as we ask God's blessing for ourselves individually, so let us hope and pray that the National Church may be drawn into a closer union, and be led into a more life-like activity, not for the mere purposes of self-preservation and self-defence, but for the grander and more Christian object of assailing the common enemies of humanity. Then, and not till then, will the signs of the Church appear again, and poor and rich will worship side by side, adoring the common Father; social quarrels will subside; religious difficulties vanish, and the English Church will be identical with the English nation.

LONDON:
R. CLAY, SONS, AND TAYLOR, PRINTERS,
BREAD STREET HILL.

June 1874.

A Catalogue of Theological Books, with a Short Account of their Character and Aim,

Published by

MACMILLAN AND CO.

Bedford Street, Strand, London, W.C.

Abbott (Rev. E. A.)—Works by the Rev. E. A. ABBOTT, D.D., Head Master of the City of London School.

BIBLE LESSONS. Second Edition. Crown 8vo. 4s. 6d.

"*Wise, suggestive, and really profound initiation into religious thought.*"—Guardian. *The Bishop of St. David's, in his speech at the Education Conference at Abergwilly, says he thinks "nobody could read them without being the better for them himself, and being also able to see how this difficult duty of imparting a sound religious education may be effected."*

THE GOOD VOICES: A Child's Guide to the Bible. With upwards of 50 Illustrations. Crown 8vo. cloth gilt. 5s.

"*It would not be easy to combine simplicity with fulness and depth of meaning more successfully than Mr. Abbott has done.*"—Spectator. *The* Times *says*—"*Mr. Abbott writes with clearness, simplicity, and the deepest religious feeling.*"

PARABLES FOR CHILDREN. Crown 8vo. cloth gilt. 3s. 6d.

"*They are simple and direct in meaning and told in plain language, and are therefore well adapted to their purpose.*"—Guardian.

THEOLOGICAL BOOKS.

Ainger (Rev. Alfred).—SERMONS PREACHED IN THE TEMPLE CHURCH. By the Rev. ALFRED AINGER, M.A. of Trinity Hall, Cambridge, Reader at the Temple Church. Extra fcap. 8vo. 6s.

This volume contains twenty-four Sermons preached at various times during the last few years in the Temple Church. "It is," the British Quarterly says, "the fresh unconventional talk of a clear independent thinker, addressed to a congregation of thinkers.... Thoughtful men will be greatly charmed by this little volume."

Alexander.—THE LEADING IDEAS of the GOSPELS. Five Sermons preached before the University of Oxford in 1870—71. By WILLIAM ALEXANDER, D.D., Brasenose College; Lord Bishop of Derry and Raphoe; Select Preacher. Cr. 8vo. 4s. 6d.

"Eloquence and force of language, clearness of statement, and a hearty appreciation of the grandeur and importance of the topics upon which he writes characterize his sermons."—Record.

Arnold.—A BIBLE READING BOOK FOR SCHOOLS. THE GREAT PROPHECY OF ISRAEL'S RESTORATION (Isaiah, Chapters 40—66). Arranged and Edited for Young Learners. By MATTHEW ARNOLD, D.C.L., formerly Professor of Poetry in the University of Oxford, and Fellow of Oriel. Third Edition. 18mo. cloth. 1s.

The Times says—"Whatever may be the fate of this little book in Government Schools, there can be no doubt that it will be found excellently calculated to further instruction in Biblical literature in any school into which it may be introduced.... We can safely say that whatever school uses this book, it will enable its pupils to understand Isaiah, a great advantage compared with other establishments which do not avail themselves of it."

Baring-Gould.—LEGENDS OF OLD TESTAMENT CHARACTERS, from the Talmud and other sources. By the Rev. S. BARING-GOULD, M.A., Author of "Curious Myths of the Middle Ages," "The Origin and Development of Religious Belief," "In Exitu Israel," etc. In two vols. crown 8vo. 16s. Vol. I. Adam to Abraham. Vol. II. Melchizidek to Zechariah.

He has collected from the Talmud and other sources, Jewish and Mahommedan, a large number of curious and interesting legends concerning the principal characters of the Old Testament, comparing these frequently with similar legends current among many of the peoples, savage and civilised, all over the world. "These volumes contain much that is strange, and to the ordinary English reader, very novel."—Daily News.

Barry, Alfred, D.D.—The ATONEMENT of CHRIST. Six Lectures delivered in Hereford Cathedral during Holy Week, 1871. By ALFRED BARRY, D.D., D.C.L., Canon of Worcester, Principal of King's College, London. Fcap. 8vo. 2s. 6d.

In writing these Sermons, it has been the object of Canon Barry to set forth the deep practical importance of the doctrinal truths of the Atonement. "The one truth," says the Preface, "which, beyond all others, I desire that these may suggest, is the inseparable unity which must exist between Christian doctrine, even in its more mysterious forms, and Christian morality or devotion. They are a slight contribution to the plea of that connection of Religion and Theology, which in our own time is so frequently and, as it seems to me, so unreasonably denied." The Guardian *calls them "striking and eloquent lectures."*

Benham.—A COMPANION TO THE LECTIONARY, being a Commentary on the Proper Lessons for Sundays and Holydays. By the Rev. W. BENHAM, B.D., Vicar of Margate. Crown 8vo. 7s. 6d.

The Author's object is to give the reader a clear understanding of the Lessons of the Church, which he does by means of general and special introductions, and critical and explanatory notes on all words and passages presenting the least difficulty. "A very useful book. Mr. Benham has produced a good and welcome companion to our revised Lectionary. Its contents will, if not very original or profound, prove to be sensible and practical, and often suggestive to the preacher and the Sunday School teacher. They will also furnish some excellent Sunday reading for private hours."—Guardian.

Bernard.—THE PROGRESS OF DOCTRINE IN THE NEW TESTAMENT, considered in Eight Lectures before the University of Oxford in 1864. By THOMAS D. BERNARD, M.A., Rector of Walcot and Canon of Wells. Third and Cheaper Edition. Crown 8vo. 5s. (Bampton Lectures for 1864.)

"We lay down these lectures with a sense not only of being edified by sound teaching and careful thought, but also of being gratified by conciseness and clearness of expression and elegance of style."—Churchman.

Binney.—SERMONS PREACHED IN THE KING'S WEIGH HOUSE CHAPEL, 1829—69. By THOMAS BINNEY, D.D. New and Cheaper Edition. Extra fcap. 8vo. 4s. 6d.

"Full of robust intelligence, of reverent but independent thinking on the most profound and holy themes, and of earnest practical purpose."—London Quarterly Review.

Bradby.—SERMONS PREACHED AT HAILEYBURY. By E. H. BRADBY, M.A., Master. 8vo. 10s. 6d.

"He who claims a public hearing now, speaks to an audience accustomed to Cotton, Temple, Vaughan, Bradley, Butler, Farrar, and others...... Each has given us good work, several work of rare beauty, force, or originality; but we doubt whether any one of them has touched deeper chords, or brought more freshness and strength into his sermons, than the last of their number, the present Head Master of Haileybury."—Spectator.

Burgon.—A TREATISE on the PASTORAL OFFICE. Addressed chiefly to Candidates for Holy Orders, or to those who have recently undertaken the cure of souls. By the Rev. JOHN W. BURGON, M.A., Oxford. 8vo. 12s.

The object of this work is to expound the great ends to be accomplished by the Pastoral office, and to investigate the various means by which these ends may best be gained. Full directions are given as to preaching and sermon-writing, pastoral visitation, village education and catechising, and confirmation.—Spectator.

Butler (G.)—Works by the Rev. GEORGE BUTLER, M.A., Principal of Liverpool College:

FAMILY PRAYERS. Crown 8vo. 5s.

The prayers in this volume are all based on passages of Scripture—the morning prayers on Select Psalms, those for the evening on portions of the New Testament.

SERMONS PREACHED in CHELTENHAM COLLEGE CHAPEL. Crown 8vo. 7s. 6d.

Butler (Rev. H. M.)—SERMONS PREACHED in the CHAPEL OF HARROW SCHOOL. By H. MONTAGU BUTLER, Head Master. Crown 8vo. 7s. 6d.

"*These sermons are adapted for every household. There is nothing more striking than the excellent good sense with which they are imbued.*" -Spectator.

A SECOND SERIES. Crown 8vo. 7s. 6d.

"*Excellent specimens of what sermons should be,—plain, direct, practical, pervaded by the true spirit of the Gospel, and holding up lofty aims before the minds of the young.*"—Athenæum.

Butler (Rev. W. Archer).—Works by the Rev. WILLIAM ARCHER BUTLER, M.A., late Professor of Moral Philosophy in the University of Dublin:—

SERMONS, DOCTRINAL AND PRACTICAL. Edited, with a Memoir of the Author's Life, by THOMAS WOODWARD, Dean of Down. With Portrait. Ninth Edition. 8vo. 8s.

The Introductory Memoir narrates in considerable detail and with much interest, the events of Butler's brief life; and contains a few specimens of his poetry, and a few extracts from his addresses and essays, including a long and eloquent passage on the Province and Duty of the Preacher.

A SECOND SERIES OF SERMONS. Edited by J. A. JEREMIE, D.D., Dean of Lincoln. Seventh Edition. 8vo. 7s.

The North British Review *says,* "*Few sermons in our language exhibit the same rare combination of excellencies; imagery almost as rich as Taylor's; oratory as vigorous often as South's; judgment as sound as*

Butler (Rev. W. Archer.)—*continued.*
Barrow's; a style as attractive but more copious, original, and forcible than Atterbury's; piety as elevated as Howe's, and a fervour as intense at times as Baxter's. Mr. Butler's are the sermons of a true poet."

LETTERS ON ROMANISM, in reply to Dr. Newman's Essay on Development. Edited by the Dean of Down. Second Edition, revised by Archdeacon HARDWICK. 8vo. 10s. 6d.

These Letters contain an exhaustive criticism of Dr. Newman's famous "Essay on the Development of Christian Doctrine." "A work which ought to be in the Library of every student of Divinity."—BP. ST. DAVID'S.

LECTURES ON ANCIENT PHILOSOPHY. *See* SCIENTIFIC CATALOGUE.

Cambridge Lent Sermons.—SERMONS preached during Lent, 1864, in Great St. Mary's Church, Cambridge. By the BISHOP OF OXFORD, Revs. H. P. LIDDON, T. L. CLAUGHTON, J. R. WOODFORD, Dr. GOULBURN, J. W. BURGON, T. T. CARTER, Dr. PUSEY, Dean HOOK, W. J. BUTLER, Dean GOODWIN. Crown 8vo. 7s. 6d.

Campbell.—Works by JOHN M'LEOD CAMPBELL :—

THE NATURE OF THE ATONEMENT AND ITS RELATION TO REMISSION OF SINS AND ETERNAL LIFE. Fourth and Cheaper Edition, crown 8vo. 6s.

"Among the first theological treatises of this generation."—Guardian.
"One of the most remarkable theological books ever written."—Times.

CHRIST THE BREAD OF LIFE. An Attempt to give a profitable direction to the present occupation of Thought with Romanism. Second Edition, greatly enlarged. Crown 8vo. 4s. 6d.

"Deserves the most attentive study by all who interest themselves in the predominant religious controversy of the day."—Spectator.

RESPONSIBILITY FOR THE GIFT OF ETERNAL LIFE. Compiled by permission of the late J. M'LEOD CAMPBELL, D.D., from Sermons preached chiefly at Row in 1829—31. Crown 8vo. 5s.

"There is a healthy tone as well as a deep pathos not often seen in sermons. His words are weighty and the ideas they express tend to perfection of life."—Westminster Review.

REMINISCENCES AND REFLECTIONS, referring to his Early Ministry in the Parish of Row, 1825—31. Edited with an Introductory Narrative by his Son, DONALD CAMPBELL, M.A., Chaplain of King's College, London. Crown 8vo. 7s. 6d.

These 'Reminiscences and Reflections,' written during the last year of his life, were mainly intended to place on record thoughts which might

prove helpful to others. "We recommend this book cordially to all who are interested in the great cause of religious reformation."—Times.
"There is a thoroughness and depth, as well as a practical earnestness, in his grasp of each truth on which he dilates, which make his reflections very valuable."—Literary Churchman.

Canterbury.—THE PRESENT POSITION OF THE CHURCH OF ENGLAND. Seven Addresses delivered to the Clergy and Churchwardens of his Diocese, as his Charge, at his Primary Visitation, 1872. By ARCHIBALD CAMPBELL, Archbishop of Canterbury. Third Edition. 8vo. cloth. 3s. 6d.

The subjects of these Addresses are, I. Lay Co-operation. II. Cathedral Reform. III. and IV. Ecclesiastical Judicature. V. Ecclesiastical Legislation. VI. Missionary Work of the Church. VII. The Church of England in its relation to the Rest of Christendom. There are besides, a number of statistical and illustrative appendices.

Cheyne.—Works by T. K. CHEYNE, M.A., Fellow of Balliol College, Oxford:—

THE BOOK OF ISAIAH CHRONOLOGICALLY ARRANGED. An Amended Version, with Historical and Critical Introductions and Explanatory Notes. Crown 8vo. 7s. 6d.

The object of this edition is to restore the probable meaning of Isaiah, so far as can be expressed in appropriate English. The basis of the version is the revised translation of 1611, *but alterations have been introduced wherever the true sense of the prophecies appeared to require it. The* Westminster Review *speaks of it as "a piece of scholarly work, very carefully and considerately done." The* Academy *calls it "a successful attempt to extend a right understanding of this important Old Testament writing."*

NOTES AND CRITICISMS on the HEBREW TEXT OF ISAIAH. Crown 8vo. 2s. 6d.

This work is offered as a slight contribution to a more scientific study of the Old Testament Scriptures. The author aims at completeness, independence, and originality, and constantly endeavours to keep philology distinct from exegesis, to explain the form without pronouncing on the matter.

Choice Notes on the Four Gospels, drawn from Old and New Sources. Crown 8vo. 4s. 6d. each Vol. (St. Matthew and St. Mark in one Vol. price 9s.).

These Notes are selected from the Rev. Prebendary Ford's Illustrations of the Four Gospels, the choice being chiefly confined to those of a more simple and practical character.

Church.—Works by the Very Rev. R. W. CHURCH, M.A., Dean of St. Paul's.

SERMONS PREACHED BEFORE the UNIVERSITY OF OXFORD. By the Very Rev. R. W. CHURCH, M.A., Dean of St. Paul's. Second Edition. Crown 8vo. 4s. 6d.

Sermons on the relations between Christianity and the ideas and facts of modern civilized society. The subjects of the various discourses are:—"The Gifts of Civilization," "Christ's Words and Christian Society," "Christ's Example," and "Civilization and Religion." "Thoughtful and masterly... We regard these sermons as a landmark in religious thought. They help us to understand the latent strength of a Christianity that is assailed on all sides."—Spectator.

ON SOME INFLUENCES OF CHRISTIANITY UPON NATIONAL CHARACTER. Three Lectures delivered in St. Paul's Cathedral, Feb. 1873. Crown 8vo. 4s. 6d.

"Few books that we have met with have given us keener pleasure than this....... It would be a real pleasure to quote extensively, so wise and so true, so tender and so discriminating are Dean Church's judgments, but the limits of our space are inexorable. We hope the book will be bought." —Literary Churchman.

THE SACRED POETRY OF EARLY RELIGIONS. Two Lectures in St. Paul's Cathedral. 18mo. 1s. I. The Vedas. II. The Psalms.

Clay.—THE POWER OF THE KEYS. Sermons preached in Coventry. By the Rev. W. L. CLAY, M.A. Fcap. 8vo. 3s. 6d.

In this work an attempt is made to shew in what sense, and to what extent, the power of the Keys can be exercised by the layman, the Church, and the priest respectively. The Church Review *says the sermons are "in many respects of unusual merit."*

Clergyman's Self-Examination concerning the
APOSTLES' CREED. Extra fcap. 8vo. 1s. 6d.

Collects of the Church of England.
With a beautifully Coloured Floral Design to each Collect, and Illuminated Cover. Crown 8vo. 12s. Also kept in various styles of morocco.

The distinctive characteristic of this edition is the coloured floral design which accompanies each Collect, and which is generally emblematical of the character of the day or saint to which it is assigned; the flowers which have been selected are such as are likely to be in bloom on the day to which the Collect belongs. The Guardian *thinks it "a successful attempt to associate in a natural and unforced manner the flowers of our fields and gardens with the course of the Christian year."*

Cotton.—Works by the late GEORGE EDWARD LYNCH COTTON, D.D., Bishop of Calcutta:—

SERMONS PREACHED TO ENGLISH CONGREGATIONS IN INDIA. Crown 8vo. 7s. 6d.

"*The sermons are models of what sermons should be, not only on account of their practical teachings, but also with regard to the singular felicity with which they are adapted to times, places, and circumstances.*"—Spectator.

EXPOSITORY SERMONS ON THE EPISTLES FOR THE SUNDAYS OF THE CHRISTIAN YEAR. Two Vols. Crown 8vo. 15s.

These two volumes contain in all fifty-seven Sermons. They were all preached at various stations throughout India.

Cure.—THE SEVEN WORDS OF CHRIST ON THE CROSS. Sermons preached at St. George's, Bloomsbury. By the Rev. E. CAPEL CURE, M.A. Fcap. 8vo. 3s. 6d.

Of these Sermons the John Bull *says,* "*They are earnest and practical;*" *the* Nonconformist, "*The Sermons are beautiful, tender, and instructive;*" *and the* Spectator *calls them* "*A set of really good Sermons.*"

Curteis.—DISSENT in its RELATION to the CHURCH OF ENGLAND. Eight Lectures preached before the University of Oxford, in the year 1871, on the foundation of the late Rev. John Bampton, M.A., Canon of Salisbury. By GEORGE HERBERT CURTEIS, M.A., late Fellow and Sub-Rector of Exeter College; Principal of the Lichfield Theological College, and Prebendary of Lichfield Cathedral; Rector of Turweston, Bucks. Third and Cheaper Edition, crown 8vo. 7s. 6d.

"*Mr. Curteis has done good service by maintaining in an eloquent, temperate, and practical manner, that discussion among Christians is really an evil, and that an intelligent basis can be found for at least a proximate union.*"—Saturday Review "*A well timed, learned, and thoughtful book.*"

Davies.—Works by the Rev. J. LLEWELYN DAVIES, M.A., Rector of Christ Church, St. Marylebone, etc.:—

THE WORK OF CHRIST; or, the World Reconciled to God. With a Preface on the Atonement Controversy. Fcap. 8vo. 6s.

SERMONS on the MANIFESTATION OF THE SON OF GOD. With a Preface addressed to Laymen on the present Position of the Clergy of the Church of England; and an Ap-

Davies (Rev. J. Llewelyn)—*continued*.

pendix on the Testimony of Scripture and the Church as to the possibility of Pardon in the Future State. Fcap. 8vo. 6s. 6d.

"*This volume, both in its substance, prefix, and suffix, represents the noblest type of theology now preached in the English Church.*"—Spectator.

BAPTISM, CONFIRMATION, AND THE LORD'S SUPPER, as Interpreted by their Outward Signs. Three Expository Addresses for Parochial use. Fcap. 8vo., limp cloth. 1s. 6d.

The method adopted in these addresses is to set forth the natural and historical meaning of the signs of the two Sacraments and of Confirmation, and thus to arrive at the spiritual realities which they symbolize. The work touches on all the principal elements of a Christian man's faith.

THE EPISTLES of ST. PAUL TO THE EPHESIANS, THE COLOSSIANS, and PHILEMON. With Introductions and Notes, and an Essay on the Traces of Foreign Elements in the Theology of these Epistles. 8vo. 7s. 6d.

MORALITY ACCORDING TO THE SACRAMENT OF THE LORD'S SUPPER. Crown 8vo. 3s. 6d.

These discourses were preached before the University of Cambridge. They form a continuous exposition, and are directed mainly against the two-fold danger which at present threatens the Church—the tendency, on the one hand, to regard Morality as independent of Religion, and, on the other, to ignore the fact that Religion finds its proper sphere and criterion in the moral life.

THE GOSPEL and MODERN LIFE. Sermons on some of the Difficulties of the Present Day, with a Preface on a Recent Phase of Deism. Extra fcap. 8vo. 6s.

The "recent phase of Deism" examined in the preface to this volume is that professed by the "Pall Mall Gazette"—that in the sphere of Religion there are one or two "probable suppositions," but nothing more. Amongst other subjects examined are—"*Christ and Modern Knowledge,*" "*Humanity and the Trinity,*" "*Nature,*" "*Religion,*" "*Conscience,*" "*Human Corruption,*" *and* "*Human Holiness.*"

WARNINGS AGAINST SUPERSTITION IN FOUR SERMONS FOR THE DAY. Extra fcap. 8vo. 2s. 6d

"*We have seldom read a wiser little book. The Sermons are short, terse, and full of true spiritual wisdom, expressed with a lucidity and a moderation that must give them weight even with those who agree least with their author....... Of the volume as a whole it is hardly possible to speak with too cordial an appreciation.*"—Spectator.

THEOLOGICAL BOOKS.

De Teissier.—Works by G. F. DE TEISSIER, B.D.:—
VILLAGE SERMONS, FIRST SERIES. Crown 8vo. 9s.
This volume contains fifty-four short Sermons, embracing many subjects of practical importance to all Christians. The Guardian *says they are " a little too scholarlike in style for a country village, but sound and practical."*

VILLAGE SERMONS, SECOND SERIES. Crown 8vo. 8s. 6d.
" This second volume of Parochial Sermons is given to the public in the humble hope that it may afford many seasonable thoughts for such as are Mourners in Zion." There are in all fifty-two Sermons embracing a wide variety of subjects connected with Christian faith and practice.

Donaldson.—THE APOSTOLICAL FATHERS: a Critical Account of their Genuine Writings and of their Doctrines. By JAMES DONALDSON, LL.D. Crown 8vo. 7s. 6d.
This book was published in 1864 as the first volume of a 'Critical History of Christian Literature and Doctrine from the death of the Apostles to the Nicene Council.' The intention was to carry down the history continuously to the time of Eusebius, and this intention has not been abandoned. But as the writers can be sometimes grouped more easily according to subject or locality than according to time, it is deemed advisable to publish the history of each group separately. The Introduction to the present volume serves as an introduction to the whole period.

Ecce Homo. A SURVEY OF THE LIFE AND WORK OF JESUS CHRIST. Eleventh Edition. Crown 8vo. 6s.
"A very original and remarkable book, full of striking thought and delicate perception: a book which has realised with wonderful vigour and freshness the historical magnitude of Christ's work, and which here and there gives us readings of the finest kind of the probable motive of His individual words and actions."—Spectator. *" The best and most established believer will find it adding some fresh buttresses to his faith."*—Literary Churchman. *" If we have not misunderstood him, we have before us a writer who has a right to claim deference from those who think deepest and know most."*—Guardian.

Faber.—SERMONS AT A NEW SCHOOL. By the Rev. ARTHUR FABER, M.A., Head Master of Malvern College. Cr. 8vo. 6s.
" These are high-toned, earnest Sermons, orthodox and scholarlike, and laden with encouragement and warning, wisely adapted to the needs of school-life."—Literary Churchman. *"Admirably realizing that combination of fresh vigorous thought and simple expression of wise parental counsel, with brotherly sympathy and respect, which are essential to the success of such sermons, and to which so few attain."*—British Quarterly Review.

Farrar.—Works by the Rev. F. W. FARRAR, M.A., F.R.S., Head Master of Marlborough College, and Hon. Chaplain to the Queen:—

THE FALL OF MAN, AND OTHER SERMONS. Second and Cheaper Edition. Extra fcap. 8vo. 4s. 6d.

This volume contains twenty Sermons. No attempt is made in these Sermons to develope a system of doctrine. In each discourse some one aspect of truth is taken up, the chief object being to point out its bearings on practical religious life. The Nonconformist *says of these Sermons,—" Mr. Farrar's Sermons are almost perfect specimens of one type of Sermons, which we may concisely call beautiful. The style of expression is beautiful—there is beauty in the thoughts, the illustrations, the allusions—they are expressive of genuinely beautiful perceptions and feelings." The* British Quarterly *says,—"Ability, eloquence, scholarship, and practical usefulness, are in these Sermons combined in a very unusual degree."*

THE WITNESS OF HISTORY TO CHRIST. Being the Hulsean Lectures for 1870. New Edition. Crown 8vo. 5s.

The following are the subjects of the Five Lectures:—I. "The Antecedent Credibility of the Miraculous." II. "The Adequacy of the Gospel Records." III. "The Victories of Christianity." IV. "Christianity and the Individual." V. "Christianity and the Race." The subjects of the four Appendices are:—A. "The Diversity of Christian Evidences." B. "Confucius." C. "Buddha." D. "Comte."

SEEKERS AFTER GOD. The Lives of Seneca, Epictetus, and Marcus Aurelius. *See* SUNDAY LIBRARY at end of Catalogue.

THE SILENCE AND VOICES OF GOD: University and other Sermons. Crown 8vo. 6s.

"We can most cordially recommend Dr. Farrar's singularly beautiful volume of Sermons...... For beauty of diction, felicity of style, aptness of illustration and earnest loving exhortation, the volume is without its parallel."—John Bull. *"They are marked by great ability, by an honesty which does not hesitate to acknowledge difficulties and by an earnestness which commands respect."*—Pall Mall Gazette.

Fellowship: LETTERS ADDRESSED TO MY SISTER MOURNERS. Fcap. 8vo. cloth gilt. 3s. 6d.

"A beautiful little volume, written with genuine feeling, good taste, and a right appreciation of the teaching of Scripture relative to sorrow and suffering."—Nonconformist. *"A very touching, and at the same time a very sensible book. It breathes throughout the truest Christian spirit."*—Contemporary Review.

Forbes.—THE VOICE OF GOD IN THE PSALMS. By GRANVILLE FORBES, Rector of Broughton. Cr. 8vo. 6s. 6d.

Gifford.—THE GLORY OF GOD IN MAN. By E. H. GIFFORD, D.D. Fcap. 8vo., cloth. 3s. 6d.

Golden Treasury Psalter. *See* p. 27.

Hardwick.—Works by the Ven. ARCHDEACON HARDWICK:

CHRIST AND OTHER MASTERS. A Historical Inquiry into some of the Chief Parallelisms and Contrasts between Christianity and the Religious Systems of the Ancient World. New Edition, revised, and a Prefatory Memoir by the Rev. FRANCIS PROCTER, M.A. Two vols. crown 8vo. 15s.

After several introductory chapters dealing with the religious tendencies of the present age, the unity of the human race, and the characteristics of Religion under the Old Testament, the Author proceeds to consider the Religions of India, China, America, Oceanica, Egypt, and Medo-Persia. The history and characteristics of these Religions are examined, and an effort is made to bring out the points of difference and affinity between them and Christianity. The object is to establish the perfect adaptation of the latter faith to human nature in all its phases and at all times. "The plan of the work is boldly and almost nobly conceived..... We commend the work to the perusal of all those who take interest in the study of ancient mythology, without losing their reverence for the supreme authority of the oracles of the living God."—Christian Observer.

A HISTORY OF THE CHRISTIAN CHURCH. Middle Age. From Gregory the Great to the Excommunication of Luther, Edited by WILLIAM STUBBS, M.A., Regius Professor of Modern History in the University of Oxford. With Four Maps constructed for this work by A. KEITH JOHNSTON. Third Edition. Crown 8vo. 10s. 6d.

For this edition Professor Stubbs has carefully revised both text and notes, making such corrections of facts, dates, and the like as the results of recent research warrant. The doctrinal, historical, and generally speculative views of the late author have been preserved intact. "As a Manual for the student of ecclesiastical history in the Middle Ages, we know no English work which can be compared to Mr. Hardwick's book."—Guardian.

A HISTORY of the CHRISTIAN CHURCH DURING THE REFORMATION. New Edition, revised by Professor STUBBS. Crown 8vo. 10s. 6d.

This volume is intended as a sequel and companion to the "History of the Christian Church during the Middle Age." The author's earnest wish has been to give the reader a trustworthy version of those stirring incidents which mark the Reformation period, without relinquishing his former claim to characterise peculiar systems, persons, and events according to the shades and colours they assume, when contemplated from an English point of view, and by a member of the Church of England.

Hervey.—THE GENEALOGIES OF OUR LORD AND SAVIOUR JESUS CHRIST, as contained in the Gospels of St. Matthew and St. Luke, reconciled with each other, and shown to be in harmony with the true Chronology of the Times. By Lord ARTHUR HERVEY, Bishop of Bath and Wells. 8vo. 10s. 6d.

Hymni Ecclesiæ.—Fcap. 8vo. 7s. 6d.

A selection of Latin Hymns of the Mediæval Church, containing selections from the Paris Breviary, and the Breviaries of Rome, Salisbury, and York. The selection is confined to such holy days and seasons as are recognised by the Church of England, and to special events or things recorded in Scripture. This collection was edited by Dr. Newman while he lived at Oxford.

Kempis, Thos. A.—DE IMITATIONE CHRISTI. LIBRI IV. Borders in the Ancient Style, after Holbein, Durer, and other Old Masters, containing Dances of Death, Acts of Mercy, Emblems, and a variety of curious ornamentations. In white cloth, extra gilt. 7s. 6d.

The original Latin text has been here faithfully reproduced. The Spectator *says of this edition, it "has many solid merits, and is perfect in its way." While the* Athenæum *says, "The whole work is admirable; some of the figure compositions have extraordinary merit."*

Kingsley.—Works by the Rev. CHARLES KINGSLEY, M.A., Rector of Eversley, and Canon of Westminster. (For other Works by the same author, *see* HISTORICAL and BELLES LETTRES CATALOGUES).

THE WATER OF LIFE, AND OTHER SERMONS. Second Edition. Fcap. 8vo. 3s. 6d.

This volume contains twenty-one Sermons preached at various places —Westminster Abbey, Chapel Royal, before the Queen at Windsor, etc.

VILLAGE SERMONS. Seventh Edition. Fcap. 8vo. 3s. 6d.

THE GOSPEL OF THE PENTATEUCH. Second Edition. Fcap. 8vo. 3s. 6d.

This volume consists of eighteen Sermons on passages taken from the Pentateuch. They are dedicated to Dean Stanley out of gratitude for his Lectures on the Jewish Church, under the influence and in the spirit of which they were written.

GOOD NEWS OF GOD. Fourth Edition. Fcap. 8vo. 3s. 6d.

This volume contains thirty-nine short Sermons, preached in the ordinary course of the author's parochial ministrations.

Kingsley (Rev. C.)—*continued.*

SERMONS FOR THE TIMES. Third Edition. Fcap. 8vo. 3s. 6d.

Here are twenty-two Sermons, all bearing more or less on the every-day life of the present day, including such subjects as these:—"Fathers and Children;" "A Good Conscience;" "Names;" "Sponsorship;" "Duty and Superstition;" "England's Strength;" "The Lord's Prayer;" "Shame;" "Forgiveness;" "The True Gentleman;" "Public Spirit."

TOWN AND COUNTRY SERMONS. Second Edition. Extra fcap. 8vo. 3s. 6d.

Some of these Sermons were preached before the Queen, and some in the performance of the writer's ordinary parochial duty. Of these Sermons the Nonconformist *says, "They are warm with the fervour of the preacher's own heart, and strong from the force of his own convictions. There is nowhere an attempt at display, and the clearness and simplicity of the style make them suitable for the youngest or most unintelligent of his hearers."*

SERMONS on NATIONAL SUBJECTS. Second Edition. Fcap. 8vo. 3s. 6d.

THE KING OF THE EARTH, and other Sermons, a Second Series of Sermons on National Subjects. Second Edition. Fcap. 8vo. 3s. 6d.

The following extract from the Preface to the 2nd Series will explain the preacher's aim in these Sermons:—"I have tried......to proclaim the Lord Jesus Christ, as the Scriptures, both in their strictest letter and in their general method, from Genesis to Revelation, seem to me to proclaim Him; not merely as the Saviour of a few elect souls, but as the light and life of every human being who enters into the world; as the source of all reason, strength, and virtue in heathen or in Christian; as the King and Ruler of the whole universe, and of every nation, family, and man on earth; as the Redeemer of the whole earth and the whole human race... His death, as a full, perfect, and sufficient sacrifice, oblation, and satisfaction for the sins of the whole world, by which God is reconciled to the whole human race."

DISCIPLINE, AND OTHER SERMONS. Fcp. 8vo. 3s. 6d.

Twenty-four Sermons preached on various occasions, some of them of a public nature—at the Volunteer Camp, Wimbledon, before the Prince of Wales at Sandringham, at Wellington College, etc. The Guardian *says, —"There is much thought, tenderness, and devoutness of spirit in these Sermons, and some of them are models both in matter and expression."*

DAVID. FOUR SERMONS: David's Weakness—David's Strength—David's Anger—David's Deserts. Fcap. 8vo. 2s. 6d.

These four Sermons were preached before the University of Cambridge,

Kingsley (Rev. C.)—*continued.*
and are specially addressed to young men. Their titles are,—"David's Weakness;" "David's Strength;" "David's Anger;" "David's Deserts."

WESTMINSTER SERMONS. 8vo. 10s. 6d.
These Sermons were preached at Westminster Abbey or at one of the Chapels Royal. Their subjects are:—The Mystery of the Cross: The Perfect Love: The Spirit of Whitsuntide: Prayer: The Deaf and Dumb: The Fruits of the Spirit: Confusion: The Shaking of the Heavens and the Earth: The Kingdom of God: The Law of the Lord: God the Teacher: The Reasonable Prayer: The One Escape: The Word of God: I: The Cedars of Lebanon: Life: Death: Signs and Wonders: The Judgments of God: The War in Heaven: Noble Company: De Profundis: The Blessing and the Curse: The Silence of Faith: God and Mammon: The Beatific Vision.

Lightfoot.—Works by J. B. LIGHTFOOT, D.D., Hulsean Professor of Divinity in the University of Cambridge; Canon of St. Paul's.

ST. PAUL'S EPISTLE TO THE GALATIANS. A Revised Text, with Introduction, Notes, and Dissertations. Fourth Edition, revised. 8vo. cloth. 12s.

While the Author's object has been to make this commentary generally complete, he has paid special attention to everything relating to St. Paul's personal history and his intercourse with the Apostles and Church of the Circumcision, as it is this feature in the Epistle to the Galatians which has given it an overwhelming interest in recent theological controversy. The Spectator *says "there is no commentator at once of sounder judgment and more liberal than Dr. Lightfoot."*

ST. PAUL'S EPISTLE TO THE PHILIPPIANS. A Revised Text, with Introduction, Notes, and Dissertations. Third Edition. 8vo. 12s.

The plan of this volume is the same as that of " The Epistle to the Galatians." "No commentary in the English language can be compared with it in regard to fulness of information, exact scholarship, and laboured attempts to settle everything about the epistle on a solid foundation."—Athenæum.

ST. CLEMENT OF ROME, THE TWO EPISTLES TO THE CORINTHIANS. A Revised Text, with Introduction and Notes. 8vo. 8s. 6d.

This volume is the first part of a complete edition of the Apostolic Fathers. The Introductions deal with the questions of the genuineness and authenticity of the Epistles, discuss their date and character, and analyse their contents. An account is also given of all the different epistles which bear the name of Clement of Rome. "By far the most copiously annotated

Lightfoot (Dr. J. B.)—*continued.*

edition of St. Clement which we yet possess, and the most convenient in every way for the English reader."—Guardian.

ON A FRESH REVISION OF THE ENGLISH NEW TESTAMENT. Second Edition. Crown 8vo. 6s.

The Author shews in detail the necessity for a fresh revision of the authorized version on the following grounds:—1. False Readings. 2. Artificial distinctions created. 3. Real distinctions obliterated. 4. Faults of Grammar. 5. Faults of Lexicography. 6. Treatment of Proper Names, official titles, etc. 7. Archaisms, defects in the English, errors of the press, etc. *"The book is marked by careful scholarship, familiarity with the subject, sobriety, and circumspection."*—Athenæum.

Luckock.—THE TABLES OF STONE. A Course of Sermons preached in All Saints' Church, Cambridge, by H. M. LUCKOCK, M.A., Vicar. Fcap. 8vo. 3s. 6d.

Maclaren.—SERMONS PREACHED at MANCHESTER. By ALEXANDER MACLAREN. Third Edition. Fcap. 8vo. 4s. 6d.

These Sermons represent no special school, but deal with the broad principles of Christian truth, especially in their bearing on practical, every day life. A few of the titles are:—" The Stone of Stumbling," "Love and Forgiveness," " The Living Dead," "Memory in Another World," "Faith in Christ," "Love and Fear," " The Choice of Wisdom," " The Food of the World."

A SECOND SERIES OF SERMONS. Second Edition. Fcap. 8vo. 4s. 6d.

The Spectator *characterises them as "vigorous in style, full of thought, rich in illustration, and in an unusual degree interesting."*

A THIRD SERIES OF SERMONS. Second Edition. Fcap. 8vo. 4s. 6d.

Sermons more sober and yet more forcible, and with a certain wise and practical spirituality about them it would not be easy to find."—Spectator.

Maclear.—Works by G. F. MACLEAR, D.D., Head Master of King's College School:—

A CLASS-BOOK OF OLD TESTAMENT HISTORY. With Four Maps. Eighth Edition. 18mo. 4s. 6d.

"The present volume," says the Preface, "forms a Class-Book of Old Testament History from the Earliest Times to those of Ezra and Nehemiah. In its preparation the most recent authorities have been consulted, and wherever it has appeared useful, Notes have been subjoined illustrative of the Text, and, for the sake of more advanced students, references added to larger works. The Index has been so arranged as to form a concise Dictionary of the Persons and Places mentioned in the course of the

Maclear (G. F.)—*continued.*

Narrative." The Maps, prepared by Stanford, materially add to the value and usefulness of the book. The British Quarterly Review *calls it "A careful and elaborate, though brief compendium of all that modern research has done for the illustration of the Old Testament. We know of no work which contains so much important information in so small a compass."*

A CLASS-BOOK OF NEW TESTAMENT HISTORY.
Including the Connexion of the Old and New Testament. Sixth Edition. 18mo. 5s. 6d.

The present volume forms a sequel to the Author's Class-Book of Old Testament History, and continues the narrative to the close of St. Paul's second imprisonment at Rome. The work is divided into three Books—I. The Connection between the Old and New Testaments. II. The Gospel History. III. The Apostolic History. In the Appendix are given Chronological Tables The Clerical Journal *says, " It is not often that such an amount of useful and interesting matter on biblical subjects, is found in so convenient and small a compass, as in this well-arranged volume."*

A CLASS-BOOK OF THE CATECHISM OF THE CHURCH OF ENGLAND. Third and Cheaper Edition. 18mo. 1s. 6d.

The present work is intended as a sequel to the two preceding books. "Like them, it is furnished with notes and references to larger works, and it is hoped that it may be found, especially in the higher forms of our Public Schools, to supply a suitable manual of instruction in the chief doctrines of our Church, and a useful help in the preparation of Candidates for Confirmation." The Literary Churchman *says, " It is indeed the work of a scholar and divine, and as such, though extremely simple, it is also extremely instructive. There are few clergy who would not find it useful in preparing candidates for Confirmation; and there are not a few who would find it useful to themselves as well."*

A FIRST CLASS-BOOK OF THE CATECHISM OF THE CHURCH OF ENGLAND, with Scripture Proofs for Junior Classes and Schools. New Edition. 18mo. 6d.

This is an epitome of the larger Class-book, meant for junior students and elementary classes. The book has been carefully condensed, so as to contain clearly and fully, the most important part of the contents of the larger book.

A SHILLING-BOOK of OLD TESTAMENT HISTORY.
New Edition. 18mo. cloth limp. 1s.

This Manual bears the same relation to the larger Old Testament History, that the book just mentioned does to the larger work on the Catechism. It consists of Ten Books, divided into short chapters, and subdivided into

Maclear (G. F.)—*continued.*

sections, each section treating of a single episode in the history, the title of which is given in bold type.

A SHILLING-BOOK of NEW TESTAMENT HISTORY. New Edition. 18mo. cloth limp. 1s.

This bears the same relation to the larger New Testament History that the work just mentioned has to the large Old Testament History, and is marked by similar characteristics.

A MANUAL OF INSTRUCTION FOR CONFIRMATION AND FIRST COMMUNION, with Prayers and Devotions. 32mo. cloth extra, red edges. 2s.

This is an enlarged and improved edition of 'The Order of Confirmation.' To it have been added the Communion Office, with Notes and Explanations, together with a brief form of Self Examination and Devotions selected from the works of Cosin, Ken, Wilson, and others.

Macmillan.—Works by the Rev. HUGH MACMILLAN, LL.D., F.R.S.E. (For other Works by the same Author, see CATALOGUE OF TRAVELS and SCIENTIFIC CATALOGUE).

THE TRUE VINE; or, the Analogies of our Lord's Allegory. Second Edition. Globe 8vo. 6s.

This work is not merely an exposition of the fifteenth chapter of St. John's Gospel, but also a general parable of spiritual truth from the world of plants. It describes a few of the points in which the varied realm of vegetable life comes into contact with the higher spiritual realm, and shews how rich a field of promise lies before the analogical mind in this direction. The Nonconformist says, "*It abounds in exquisite bits of description, and in striking facts clearly stated.*" The British Quarterly says, "*Readers and preachers who are unscientific will find many of his illustrations as valuable as they are beautiful.*"

BIBLE TEACHINGS IN NATURE. Eighth Edition. Globe 8vo. 6s.

In this volume the author has endeavoured to shew that the teaching of nature and the teaching of the Bible are directed to the same great end; that the Bible contains the spiritual truths which are necessary to make us wise unto salvation, and the objects and scenes of nature are the pictures by which these truths are illustrated. "*He has made the world more beautiful to us, and unsealed our ears to voices of praise and messages of love that might otherwise have been unheard.*"—British Quarterly Review. "*Mr. Macmillan has produced a book which may be fitly described as one of the happiest efforts for enlisting physical science in the direct service of religion.*"—Guardian.

Macmillan (H.)—*continued.*

THE MINISTRY OF NATURE. Second Edition. Globe 8vo. 6s.

In this volume the Author attempts to interpret Nature on her religious side in accordance with the most recent discoveries of physical science, and to shew how much greater significance is imparted to many passages of Scripture and many doctrines of Christianity when looked at in the light of these discoveries. Instead of regarding Physical Science as antagonistic to Christianity, the Author believes and seeks to shew that every new discovery tends more strongly to prove that Nature and the Bible have One Author. "Whether the reader agree or not with his conclusions, he will acknowledge he is in the presence of an original and thoughtful writer."—Pall Mall Gazette. *"There is no class of educated men and women that will not profit by these essays."*—Standard.

M'Cosh.—For Works by JAMES MCCOSH, LL.D., President of Princeton College, New Jersey, U.S., *see* PHILOSOPHICAL CATALOGUE.

Maurice.—Works by the late Rev. F. DENISON MAURICE, M.A., Professor of Moral Philosophy in the University of Cambridge.

Professor Maurice's Works are recognized as having made a deep impression on modern theology. With whatever subject he dealt he tried to look at it in its bearing on living men and their every-day surroundings, and faced unshrinkingly the difficulties which occur to ordinary earnest thinkers in a manner that showed he had intense sympathy with all that concerns humanity. By all who wish to understand the various drifts of thought during the present century, Mr. Maurice's works must be studied. An intimate friend of Mr. Maurice's, one who has carefully studied all his works, and had besides many opportunities of knowing the Author's opinions, in speaking of his so-called "obscurity," ascribes it to "the never-failing assumption that God is really moving, teaching and acting: and that the writer's business is not so much to state something for the reader's benefit, as to apprehend what God is saying or doing." The Spectator *says—"Few of those of our own generation whose names will live in English history or literature have exerted so profound and so permanent an influence as Mr. Maurice."*

THE PATRIARCHS AND LAWGIVERS OF THE OLD TESTAMENT. Third and Cheaper Edition. Crown 8vo. 5s.

The Nineteen Discourses contained in this volume were preached in the chapel of Lincoln's Inn during the year 1851. The texts are taken from the books of Genesis, Exodus, Numbers, Deuteronomy, Joshua, Judges, and Samuel, and involve some of the most interesting biblical topics discussed in recent times.

Maurice (F. D.)—*continued.*

THE PROPHETS AND KINGS OF THE OLD TESTAMENT. Third Edition, with new Preface. Crown 8vo. 10s. 6d.

Mr. Maurice, in the spirit which animated the compilers of the Church Lessons, has in these Sermons regarded the Prophets more as preachers of righteousness than as mere predictors—an aspect of their lives which, he thinks, has been greatly overlooked in our day, and than which, there is none we have more need to contemplate. He has found that the Old Testament Prophets, taken in their simple natural sense, clear up many of the difficulties which beset us in the daily work of life; make the past intelligible, the present endurable, and the future real and hopeful.

THE GOSPEL OF THE KINGDOM OF HEAVEN. A Series of Lectures on the Gospel of St. Luke. Crown 8vo. 9s.

Mr. Maurice, in his Preface to these Twenty-eight Lectures, says,—"In these Lectures I have endeavoured to ascertain what is told us respecting the life of Jesus by one of those Evangelists who proclaim Him to be the Christ, who says that He did come from a Father, that He did baptize with the Holy Spirit, that He did rise from the dead. I have chosen the one who is most directly connected with the later history of the Church, who was not an Apostle, who professedly wrote for the use of a man already instructed in the faith of the Apostles. I have followed the course of the writer's narrative, not changing it under any pretext. I have adhered to his phraseology, striving to avoid the substitution of any other for his."

THE GOSPEL OF ST. JOHN. A Series of Discourses. Third and Cheaper Edition. Crown 8vo. 6s.

These Discourses, twenty-eight in number, are of a nature similar to those on the Gospel of St. Luke, and will be found to render valuable assistance to any one anxious to understand the Gospel of the beloved disciple, so different in many respects from those of the other three Evangelists. Appended are eleven notes illustrating various points which occur throughout the discourses. The Literary Churchman thus speaks of this volume:—"Thorough honesty, reverence, and deep thought pervade the work, which is every way solid and philosophical, as well as theological, and abounding with suggestions which the patient student may draw out more at length for himself."

THE EPISTLES OF ST. JOHN. A Series of Lectures on Christian Ethics. Second and Cheaper Edition. Cr. 8vo. 6s.

These Lectures on Christian Ethics were delivered to the students of the Working Men's College, Great Ormond Street, London, on a series of Sunday mornings. Mr. Maurice believes that the question in which we are most interested, the question which most affects our studies and our daily lives, is the question, whether there is a foundation for human morality,

Maurice (F. D.)—*continued.*

or whether it is dependent upon the opinions and fashions of different ages and countries. This important question will be found amply and fairly discussed in this volume, which the National Review calls "*Mr. Maurice's most effective and instructive work. He is peculiarly fitted by the constitution of his mind, to throw light on St. John's writings.*" Appended is a note on "*Positivism and its Teacher.*"

EXPOSITORY SERMONS ON THE PRAYER-BOOK. The Prayer-book considered especially in reference to the Romish System. Second Edition. Fcap. 8vo. 5s. 6d.

After an Introductory Sermon, Mr. Maurice goes over the various parts of the Church Service, expounds in eighteen Sermons, their intention and significance, and shews how appropriate they are as expressions of the deepest longings and wants of all classes of men.

LECTURES ON THE APOCALYPSE, or Book of the Revelation of St. John the Divine. Crown 8vo. 10s. 6d.

Mr. Maurice, instead of trying to find far-fetched allusions to great historical events in the distant future, endeavours to discover the plain, literal, obvious meaning of the words of the writer, and shews that as a rule these refer to events contemporaneous with or immediately succeeding the time when the book was written. At the same time he shews the applicability of the contents of the book to the circumstances of the present day and of all times. "*Never,*" says the Nonconformist, "*has Mr. Maurice been more reverent, more careful for the letter of the Scripture, more discerning of the purpose of the Spirit, or more sober and practical in his teaching, than in this volume on the Apocalypse.*"

WHAT IS REVELATION? A Series of Sermons on the Epiphany; to which are added, Letters to a Theological Student on the Bampton Lectures of Mr. Mansel. Crown 8vo. 10s. 6d.

Both Sermons and Letters were called forth by the doctrine maintained by Mr. Mansel in his Bampton Lectures, that Revelation cannot be a direct Manifestation of the Infinite Nature of God. Mr. Maurice maintains the opposite doctrine, and in his Sermons explains why, in spite of the high authorities on the other side, he must still assert the principle which he discovers in the Services of the Church and throughout the Bible.

SEQUEL TO THE INQUIRY, "WHAT IS REVELATION?" Letters in Reply to Mr. Mansel's Examination of "Strictures on the Bampton Lectures." Crown 8vo. 6s.

This, as the title indicates, was called forth by Mr. Mansel's Examination of Mr. Maurice's Strictures on his doctrine of the Infinite.

THEOLOGICAL ESSAYS. Third Edition. Crown 8vo. 10s. 6d.

"*The book,*" says Mr. Maurice, "*expresses thoughts which have been*

Maurice (F. D.)—*continued.*

working in my mind for years: the method of it has not been adopted carelessly; even the composition has undergone frequent revision." There are seventeen Essays in all, and although meant primarily for Unitarians, to quote the words of the Clerical Journal, *"it leaves untouched scarcely any topic which is in agitation in the religious world; scarcely a moot point between our various sects: scarcely a plot of debateable ground between Christians and Infidels, between Romanists and Protestants, between Socinians and other Christians, between English Churchmen and Dissenters on both sides. Scarce is there a misgiving, a difficulty, an aspiration stirring amongst us now,—now, when men seem in earnest as hardly ever before about religion, and ask and demand satisfaction with a fearlessness which seems almost awful when one thinks what is at stake—which is not recognised and grappled with by Mr. Maurice."*

THE DOCTRINE OF SACRIFICE DEDUCED FROM THE SCRIPTURES. Crown 8vo. 7s. 6d.

Throughout the Nineteen Sermons contained in this volume, Mr. Maurice expounds the ideas which he has formed of the Doctrine of Sacrifice, as it is set forth in various parts of the Bible.

THE RELIGIONS OF THE WORLD, AND THEIR RELATIONS TO CHRISTIANITY. Fourth Edition. Fcap. 8vo. 5s.

These Eight Boyle Lectures are divided into two parts, of four Lectures each. In the first part Mr. Maurice examines the great Religious systems which present themselves in the history of the world, with the purpose of inquiring what is their main characteristic principle. The second four Lectures are occupied with a discussion of the questions, "In what relation does Christianity stand to these different faiths? If there be a faith which is meant for mankind, is this the one, or must we look for another?"

ON THE LORD'S PRAYER. Fourth Edition. Fcap. 8vo. 2s. 6d.

In these Nine Sermons the successive petitions of the Lord's Prayer are taken up by Mr. Maurice, their significance expounded, and, as was usual with him, connected with the every-day lives, feelings, and aspirations of the men of the present time.

ON THE SABBATH DAY; the Character of the Warrior, and on the Interpretation of History. Fcap. 8vo. 2s. 6d.

THE GROUND AND OBJECT OF HOPE FOR MANKIND. Four Sermons preached before the University of Cambridge. Crown 8vo. 3s. 6d.

In these Four Sermons Mr. Maurice views the subject in four aspects:—I. The Hope of the Missionary. II. The Hope of the Patriot. III. The Hope of the Churchman. IV. The Hope of Man. The Spectator

Maurice (F. D.)—continued.

says, "*It is impossible to find anywhere deeper teaching than this;*" and the Nonconformist, "*We thank him for the manly, noble, stirring words in these Sermons—words fitted to quicken thoughts, to awaken high aspiration, to stimulate to lives of goodness.*"

THE LORD'S PRAYER, THE CREED, AND THE COMMANDMENTS. A Manual for Parents and Schoolmasters. To which is added the Order of the Scriptures. 18mo. cloth limp. 1s.

This book is not written for clergymen, as such, but for parents and teachers, who are often either prejudiced against the contents of the Catechism, or regard it peculiarly as the clergyman's book, but, at the same time, have a general notion that a habit of prayer ought to be cultivated, that there are some things which ought to be believed, and some things which ought to be done. It will be found to be peculiarly valuable at the present time, when the question of religious education is occupying so much attention.

THE CLAIMS OF THE BIBLE AND OF SCIENCE. A Correspondence on some Questions respecting the Pentateuch. Crown 8vo. 4s. 6d.

This volume consists of a series of Fifteen Letters, the first and last addressed by a 'Layman' to Mr. Maurice, the intervening thirteen written by Mr. Maurice himself.

DIALOGUES ON FAMILY WORSHIP. Crown 8vo. 6s.

"*The parties in these Dialogues,*" says the Preface, "*are a Clergyman who accepts the doctrines of the Church, and a Layman whose faith in them is nearly gone. The object of the Dialogues is not confutation, but the discovery of a ground on which two Englishmen and two fathers may stand, and on which their country and their children may stand when their places know them no more.*"

THE COMMANDMENTS CONSIDERED AS INSTRUMENTS OF NATIONAL REFORMATION. Crown 8vo. 4s. 6d.

The author endeavours to shew that the Commandments are now, and ever have been, the great protesters against Presbyteral and Prelatical assumptions, and that if we do not receive them as Commandments of the Lord God spoken to Israel, and spoken to every people under heaven now, we lose the greatest witnesses we possess for national morality and civil freedom.

MORAL AND METAPHYSICAL PHILOSOPHY. Vol. I. Ancient Philosophy from the First to the Thirteenth Centuries. Vol. II. Fourteenth Century and the French Revolution, with a Glimpse into the Nineteenth Century. Two Vols. 8vo. 25s.

This is an edition in two volumes of Professor Maurice's History of

Maurice (F. D.)—*continued.*

Philosophy from the earliest period to the present time. It was formerly issued in a number of separate volumes, and it is believed that all admirers of the author and all students of philosophy will welcome this compact edition. In a long introduction to this edition, in the form of a dialogue, Professor Maurice justifies his own views, and touches upon some of the most important topics of the time.

SOCIAL MORALITY. Twenty-one Lectures delivered in the University of Cambridge. New and Cheaper Edition. Cr. 8vo. 10s. 6d.

"*Whilst reading it we are charmed by the freedom from exclusiveness and prejudice, the large charity, the loftiness of thought, the eagerness to recognise and appreciate whatever there is of real worth extant in the world, which animates it from one end to the other. We gain new thoughts and new ways of viewing things, even more, perhaps, from being brought for a time under the influence of so noble and spiritual a mind.*"—Athenæum.

THE CONSCIENCE: Lectures on Casuistry, delivered in the University of Cambridge. Second and Cheaper Edition. Crown 8vo. 5s.

In this series of nine Lectures, Professor Maurice, endeavours to settle what is meant by the word "Conscience," and discusses the most important questions immediately connected with the subject. Taking "Casuistry" in its old sense as being the "study of cases of Conscience," he endeavours to show in what way it may be brought to bear at the present day upon the acts and thoughts of our ordinary existence. He shows that Conscience asks for laws, not rules; for freedom, not chains; for education, not suppression. He has abstained from the use of philosophical terms, and has touched on philosophical systems only when he fancied "they were interfering with the rights and duties of wayfarers." The Saturday Review *says: "We rise from the perusal of these lectures with a detestation of all that is selfish and mean, and with a living impression that there is such a thing as goodness after all."*

LECTURES ON THE ECCLESIASTICAL HISTORY OF THE FIRST AND SECOND CENTURIES. 8vo. 10s. 6d.

In the first chapter on "The Jewish Calling," besides expounding his idea of the true nature of a "Church," the author gives a brief sketch of the position and economy of the Jews; while in the second he points out their relation to "the other Nations." Chapter Third contains a succint account of the various Jewish Sects, while in Chapter Fourth are briefly set forth Mr. Maurice's ideas of the character of Christ and the nature of His mission, and a sketch of events is given up to the Day of Pentecost. The remaining Chapters, extending from the Apostles' personal Ministry to the end of the Second Century, contain sketches of the character and

Maurice (F. D.)—*continued.*
work of all the prominent men in any way connected with the Early Church, accounts of the origin and nature of the various doctrines orthodox and heretical which had their birth during the period, as well as of the planting and early history of the Chief Churches in Asia, Africa and Europe.

> LEARNING AND WORKING. Six Lectures delivered in Willis's Rooms, London, in June and July, 1854.—THE RELIGION OF ROME, and its Influence on Modern Civilisation. Four Lectures delivered in the Philosophical Institution of Edinburgh, in December, 1854. Crown 8vo. 5s.
>
> SERMONS PREACHED IN COUNTRY CHURCHES. Crown 8vo. 10s. 6d.
>
> "*Earnest, practical, and extremely simple.*"—Literary Churchman. "*Good specimens of his simple and earnest eloquence. The Gospel incidents are realized with a vividness which we can well believe made the common people hear him gladly. Moreover they are sermons which must have done the hearers good.*"—John Bull.

Moorhouse.—Works by JAMES MOORHOUSE, M.A., Vicar of Paddington:—

> SOME MODERN DIFFICULTIES RESPECTING the FACTS OF NATURE AND REVELATION. Fcap. 8vo. 2s. 6d.
>
> *The first of these Four Discourses is a systematic reply to the Essay of the Rev. Baden Powell on Christian Evidences in "Essays and Reviews." The fourth Sermon, on "The Resurrection," is in some measure complementary to this, and the two together are intended to furnish a tolerably complete view of modern objections to Revelation. In the second and third Sermons, on the "Temptation" and "Passion," the author has endeavoured "to exhibit the power and wonder of those great facts within the spiritual sphere, which modern theorists have especially sought to discredit."*
>
> JACOB. Three Sermons preached before the University of Cambridge in Lent 1870. Extra fcap. 8vo. 3s. 6d.
>
> THE HULSEAN LECTURES FOR 1865. Cr. 8vo. 5s.
>
> "*Few more valuable works have come into our hands for many years... a most fruitful and welcome volume.*"—Church Review.

O'Brien.—AN ATTEMPT TO EXPLAIN and ESTABLISH THE DOCTRINE OF JUSTIFICATION by FAITH ONLY. By JAMES THOMAS O'BRIEN, D.D., Bishop of Ossory. Third Edition. 8vo. 12s.

This work consists of Ten Sermons. The first four treat of the nature and mutual relations of Faith and Justification; the fifth and sixth examine the corruptions of the doctrine of Justification by Faith only, and the objections which have been urged against it. The four concluding sermons deal with the moral effects of Faith. Various Notes are added explanatory of the Author's reasoning.

Palgrave.—HYMNS. By FRANCIS TURNER PALGRAVE. Third Edition, enlarged. 18mo. 1s. 6d.

This is a collection of twenty original Hymns, which the Literary Churchman *speaks of as "so choice, so perfect, and so refined,—so tender in feeling, and so scholarly in expression."*

Paul of Tarsus. An Inquiry into the Times and the Gospel of the Apostle of the Gentiles. By a GRADUATE. 8vo. 10s. 6d.

The Author of this work has attempted, out of the materials which were at his disposal, to construct for himself a sketch of the time in which St. Paul lived, of the religious systems with which he was brought in contact, of the doctrine which he taught, and of the work which he ultimately achieved. "Turn where we will throughout the volume, we find the best fruit of patient inquiry, sound scholarship, logical argument, and fairness of conclusion. No thoughtful reader will rise from its perusal without a real and lasting profit to himself, and a sense of permanent addition to the cause of truth."—Standard.

Picton.—THE MYSTERY OF MATTER; and other Essays. By J. ALLANSON PICTON, Author of "New Theories and the Old Faith." Crown 8vo. 10s. 6d.

Contents—The Mystery of Matter: The Philosophy of Ignorance: The Antithesis of Faith and Sight: The Essential Nature of Religion: Christian Pantheism.

Prescott.—THE THREEFOLD CORD. Sermons preached before the University of Cambridge. By J. E. PRESCOTT, B.D. Fcap. 8vo. 3s. 6d.

Procter.—A HISTORY OF THE BOOK OF COMMON PRAYER: With a Rationale of its Offices. By FRANCIS PROCTER, M.A. Eleventh Edition, revised and enlarged. Crown 8vo. 10s. 6d.

The Athenæum *says:*—"*The origin of every part of the Prayer-book has been diligently investigated,—and there are few questions or facts connected with it which are not either sufficiently explained, or so referred to, that persons interested may work out the truth for themselves.*"

Procter and Maclear.—AN ELEMENTARY INTRODUCTION TO THE BOOK OF COMMON PRAYER. Re-arranged and Supplemented by an Explanation of the Morning and Evening Prayer and the Litany. By F. PROCTER, M.A. and G. F. MACLEAR, D.D. New Edition. 18mo. 2s. 6d.

This book has the same object and follows the same plan as the Manuals already noticed under Mr. Maclear's name. Each book is subdivided into chapters and sections. In Book I. is given a detailed History of the Book of Common Prayer down to the Attempted Revision in the Reign of William III. Book II., consisting of four Parts, treats in order the various parts of the Prayer Book. Notes, etymological, historical, and critical, are given throughout the book, while the Appendix contains several articles of much interest and importance. Appended is a General Index and an Index of Words explained in the Notes. The Literary Churchman *characterizes it as "by far the completest and most satisfactory book of its kind we know. We wish it were in the hands of every schoolboy and every schoolmaster in the kingdom."*

Psalms of David CHRONOLOGICALLY ARRANGED. An Amended Version, with Historical Introductions and Explanatory Notes. By FOUR FRIENDS. Second and Cheaper Edition, much enlarged. Crown 8vo. 8s. 6d.

One of the chief designs of the Editors, in preparing this volume, was to restore the Psalter as far as possible to the order in which the Psalms were written. They give the division of each Psalm into strophes, and of each strophe into the lines which composed it, and amend the errors of translation. The Spectator *calls it "One of the most instructive and valuable books that have been published for many years."*

Golden Treasury Psalter.—THE STUDENT'S EDITION. Being an Edition with briefer Notes of the above. 18mo. 3s. 6d.

This volume will be found to meet the requirements of those who wish for a smaller edition of the larger work, at a lower price for family use, and for the use of younger pupils in Public Schools. The short notes which are appended to the volume will, it is hoped, suffice to make the meaning intelligible throughout. The aim of this edition is simply to put the reader as far as possible in possession of the plain meaning of the writer. "It is a gem," the Nonconformist *says.*

Ramsay.—THE CATECHISER'S MANUAL; or, the Church Catechism Illustrated and Explained, for the Use of Clergymen, Schoolmasters, and Teachers. By ARTHUR RAMSAY, M.A. Second Edition. 18mo. 1s. 6d.

Rays of Sunlight for Dark Days. A Book of Selections for the Suffering. With a Preface by C. J. VAUGHAN, D.D. 18mo. New Edition. 3s. 6d. Also in morocco, old style.

Dr. Vaughan *says in the Preface, after speaking of the general run of Books of Comfort for Mourners, "It is because I think that the little volume now offered to the Christian sufferer is one of greater wisdom and of deeper experience, that I have readily consented to the request that I* would introduce it by a few words of Preface." *The book consists of a series of very brief extracts from a great variety of authors, in prose and poetry, suited to the many moods of a mourning or suffering mind. "Mostly gems of the first water."*—Clerical Journal.

Reynolds.—NOTES OF THE CHRISTIAN LIFE. A Selection of Sermons by HENRY ROBERT REYNOLDS, B.A., President of Cheshunt College, and Fellow of University College, London. Crown 8vo. 7s. 6d.

This work may be taken as representative of the mode of thought and feeling which is most popular amongst the freer and more cultivated Nonconformists. "It is long," says the Nonconformist, *"since we have met with any published sermons better calculated than these to stimulate devout thought, and to bring home to the soul the reality of a spiritual life."*

Roberts.—DISCUSSIONS ON THE GOSPELS. By the Rev. ALEXANDER ROBERTS, D.D. Second Edition, revised and enlarged. 8vo. 16s.

This volume is divided into two parts. Part I. "On the Language employed by our Lord and His Disciples," in which the author endeavours to prove that Greek was the language usually employed by Christ Himself, in opposition to the common belief that Our Lord spoke Aramæan. Part II. is occupied with a discussion "On the Original Language of St. Matthew's Gospel," and on "The Origin and Authenticity of the Gospels." "The author brings the valuable qualifications of learning, temper, and an independent judgment."—Daily News.

Robertson.—PASTORAL COUNSELS. Being Chapters on Practical and Devotional Subjects. By the late JOHN ROBERTSON, D.D. Third Edition, with a Preface by the Author of "The Recreations of a Country Parson." Extra fcap. 8vo. 6s.

These Sermons are the free utterances of a strong and independent thinker. He does not depart from the essential doctrines of his Church, but he expounds them in a spirit of the widest charity, and always having most prominently in view the requirements of practical life. "The sermons are admirable specimens of a practical, earnest, and instructive style of pulpit teaching."—Nonconformist.

Rowsell.—MAN'S LABOUR AND GOD'S HARVEST. Sermons preached before the University of Cambridge in Lent, 1861. Fcap. 8vo. 3s.

"We strongly recommend this little volume to young men, and especially to those who are contemplating working for Christ in Holy Orders."—Literary Churchman.

Salmon.—THE REIGN OF LAW, and other Sermons, preached in the Chapel of Trinity College, Dublin. By the Rev. GEORGE SALMON, D.D., Regius Professor of Divinity in the University of Dublin. Crown 8vo. 6s.

"Well considered, learned, and powerful discourses."—Spectator.

Sanday.—THE AUTHORSHIP AND HISTORICAL CHARACTER OF THE FOURTH GOSPEL, considered in reference to the Contents of the Gospel itself. A Critical Essay. By WILLIAM SANDAY, M.A., Fellow of Trinity College, Oxford. Crown 8vo. 8s. 6d.

The object of this Essay is critical and nothing more. The Author attempts to apply faithfully and persistently to the contents of the much disputed fourth Gospel that scientific method which has been so successful in other directions. "The facts of religion," the Author believes, "(i. e. the documents, the history of religious bodies, &c.) are as much facts as the lie of a coal-bed or the formation of a coral-reef." "The Essay is not only most valuable in itself, but full of promise for the future."—Canon Westcott in the *Academy*.

Selborne.—THE BOOK OF PRAISE: From the Best English Hymn Writers. Selected and arranged by Lord SELBORNE. With Vignette by WOOLNER. 18mo. 4s. 6d.

The present is an attempt to present, under a convenient arrangement, a collection of such examples of a copious and interesting branch of popular literature, as, after several years' study of the subject, have seemed to the Editor most worthy of being separated from the mass to which they belong. It has been the Editor's desire and aim to adhere strictly, in all cases in which it could be ascertained, to the genuine uncorrupted text of the authors themselves. The names of the authors and date of composition of the hymns, when known, are affixed, while notes are added to the volume, giving further details. The Hymns are arranged according to subjects. "There is not room for two opinions as to the value of the 'Book of Praise.'" —Guardian. *"Approaches as nearly as one can conceive to perfection."* —Nonconformist.

BOOK OF PRAISE HYMNAL. *See* end of this Catalogue.

Sergeant.—SERMONS. By the Rev. E. W. SERGEANT, M.A., Balliol College, Oxford; Assistant Master at Westminster College. Fcap. 8vo. 2s. 6d.

Smith.—PROPHECY A PREPARATION FOR CHRIST. Eight Lectures preached before the University of Oxford, being the Bampton Lectures for 1869. By R. PAYNE SMITH, D.D., Dean of Canterbury. Second and Cheaper Edition. Crown 8vo. 6s.

The author's object in these Lectures is to shew that there exists in the Old Testament an element, which no criticism on naturalistic principles can either account for or explain away: that element is Prophecy. The author endeavours to prove that its force does not consist merely in its predictions. "These Lectures overflow with solid learning."—Record.

Smith.—CHRISTIAN FAITH. Sermons preached before the University of Cambridge. By W. SAUMAREZ SMITH, M.A., Principal of St. Aidan's College, Birkenhead. Fcap. 8vo. 3s. 6d.

"*Appropriate and earnest sermons, suited to the practical exhortation of an educated congregation.*"—Guardian.

Stanley.—Works by the Very Rev. A. P. STANLEY, D.D., Dean of Westminster.

THE ATHANASIAN CREED, with a Preface on the General Recommendations of the RITUAL COMMISSION. Cr. 8vo. 2s.

The object of the work is not so much to urge the omission or change of the Athanasian Creed, as to show that such a relaxation ought to give offence to no reasonable or religious mind. With this view, the Dean of Westminster discusses in succession—(1) *the Authorship of the Creed,* (2) *its Internal Characteristics,* (3) *the Peculiarities of its Use in the Church of England,* (4) *its Advantages and Disadvantages,* (5) *its various Interpretations, and* (6) *the Judgment passed upon it by the Ritual Commission. In conclusion, Dr. Stanley maintains that the use of the Athanasian Creed should no longer be made compulsory.* "*Dr. Stanley puts with admirable force the objections which may be made to the Creed; equally admirable, we think, in his statement of its advantages.*"—Spectator.

THE NATIONAL THANKSGIVING. Sermons preached in Westminster Abbey. Second Edition. Crown 8vo. 2s. 6d.

These Sermons are (1) "*Death and Life,*" *preached December* 10, 1871; (2) "*The Trumpet of Patmos,*" *December* 17, 1871; (3) "*The Day of Thanksgiving,*" *March* 3, 1872. "*In point of fervour and polish by far the best specimens in print of Dean Stanley's eloquent style.*"—Standard.

Sunday Library. See end of this Catalogue.

Swainson.—Works by C. A. SWAINSON, D.D., Canon of Chichester:—

THE CREEDS OF THE CHURCH IN THEIR RELATIONS TO HOLY SCRIPTURE and the CONSCIENCE OF THE CHRISTIAN. 8vo. cloth. 9s.

The Lectures which compose this volume discuss, amongst others, the following subjects: "*Faith in God,*" "*Exercise of our Reason,*" "*Origin and Authority of Creeds,*" *and* "*Private Judgment, its use and exercise.*" "*Treating of abstruse points of Scripture, he applies them so forcibly to Christian duty and practice as to prove eminently serviceable to the Church.*"—John Bull.

THEOLOGICAL BOOKS. 31

Swainson (C. A.)—*continued.*

THE AUTHORITY OF THE NEW TESTAMENT, and other LECTURES, delivered before the University of Cambridge. 8vo. cloth. 12*s.*

The first series of Lectures in this work is on "The Words spoken by the Apostles of Jesus," "The Inspiration of God's Servants," "The Human Character of the Inspired Writers," and "The Divine Character of the Word written." The second embraces Lectures on "Sin as Imperfection," "Sin as Self-will," "Whatsoever is not of Faith is Sin," "Christ the Saviour," and "The Blood of the New Covenant." The third is on "Christians One Body in Christ," "The One Body the Spouse of Christ," "Christ's Prayer for Unity," "Our Reconciliation should be manifested in common Worship," and "Ambassadors for Christ."

Taylor.—THE RESTORATION OF BELIEF. New and Revised Edition. By ISAAC TAYLOR, Esq. Crown 8vo. 8*s.* 6*d.*

The earlier chapters are occupied with an examination of the primitive history of the Christian Religion, and its relation to the Roman government; and here, as well as in the remainder of the work, the author shews the bearing of that history on some of the difficult and interesting questions which have recently been claiming the attention of all earnest men. The last chapter of this New Edition treats of "The Present Position of the Argument concerning Christianity," with special reference to M. Renan's Vie de Jésus.

Temple.—SERMONS PREACHED IN THE CHAPEL of RUGBY SCHOOL. By F. TEMPLE, D.D., Bishop of Exeter. New and Cheaper Edition. Extra fcap. 8vo. 4*s.* 6*d.*

This volume contains Thirty-five Sermons on topics more or less intimately connected with every-day life. The following are a few of the subjects discoursed upon:—*"Love and Duty;" "Coming to Christ;" "Great Men;" "Faith;" "Doubts;" "Scruples;" "Original Sin;" "Friendship;" "Helping Others;" "The Discipline of Temptation;" "Strength a Duty;" "Worldliness;" "Ill Temper;" "The Burial of the Past."*

A SECOND SERIES OF SERMONS PREACHED IN THE CHAPEL OF RUGBY SCHOOL. Second Edition. Extra fcap. 8vo. 6*s.*

This Second Series of Forty-two brief, pointed, practical Sermons, on topics intimately connected with the every-day life of young and old, will be acceptable to all who are acquainted with the First Series. The following are a few of the subjects treated of:—*"Disobedience," "Almsgiving," "The Unknown Guidance of God," "Apathy one of our Trials," "High Aims in Leaders," "Doing our Best," "The Use of Knowledge," "Use of Observances," "Martha and Mary," "John the Baptist," "Severity*

Temple (F., D.D.)—*continued*.

before Mercy," "Even Mistakes Punished," "Morality and Religion," "Children," "Action the Test of Spiritual Life," "Self-Respect," "Too Late," "The Tercentenary."

A THIRD SERIES OF SERMONS PREACHED IN RUGBY SCHOOL CHAPEL IN 1867—1869. Extra fcap. 8vo. 6s.

This third series of Bishop Temple's Rugby Sermons, contains thirty-six brief discourses, including the "Good-bye" sermon preached on his leaving Rugby to enter on the office he now holds.

Thring.—Works by Rev. EDWARD THRING, M.A.

SERMONS DELIVERED AT UPPINGHAM SCHOOL. Crown 8vo. 5s.

In this volume are contained Forty-seven brief Sermons, all on subjects more or less intimately connected with Public-school life. "We desire very highly to commend these capital Sermons which treat of a boy's life and trials in a thoroughly practical way and with great simplicity and impressiveness. They deserve to be classed with the best of their kind."— Literary Churchman.

THOUGHTS ON LIFE-SCIENCE. New Edition, enlarged and revised. Crown 8vo. 7s. 6d.

In this volume are discussed in a familiar manner some of the most interesting problems between Science and Religion, Reason and Feeling.

Tracts for Priests and People. By VARIOUS WRITERS.

THE FIRST SERIES. Crown 8vo. 8s.

THE SECOND SERIES. Crown 8vo. 8s.

The whole Series of Fifteen Tracts may be had separately, price One Shilling each.

Trench.—Works by R. CHENEVIX TRENCH, D.D., Archbishop of Dublin. (For other Works by the same author, *see* BIOGRAPHICAL, BELLES LETTRES, and LINGUISTIC CATALOGUES).

NOTES ON THE PARABLES OF OUR LORD. Twelfth Edition. 8vo. 12s.

This work has taken its place as a standard exposition and interpretation of Christ's Parables. The book is prefaced by an Introductory Essay in four chapters:—I. On the definition of the Parable. II. On Teaching by Parables. III. On the Interpretation of the Parables. IV. On other Parables besides those in the Scriptures. The author then proceeds to take up the Parables one by one, and by the aid of philology, history,

Trench—*continued.*

antiquities, and the researches of travellers, shews forth the significance, beauty, and applicability of each, concluding with what he deems its true moral interpretation. In the numerous Notes are many valuable references, illustrative quotations, critical and philological annotations, etc., and appended to the volume is a classified list of fifty-six works on the Parables.

NOTES ON THE MIRACLES OF OUR LORD.
Ninth Edition. 8vo. 12s.

In the 'Preliminary Essay' to this work, all the momentous and interesting questions that have been raised in connection with Miracles, are discussed with considerable fulness. The Essay consists of six chapters:—I. On the Names of Miracles, i. e. the Greek words by which they are designated in the New Testament. II. The Miracles and Nature—What is the difference between a Miracle and any event in the ordinary course of Nature? III. The Authority of Miracles—Is the Miracle to command absolute obedience? IV. The Evangelical, compared with the other cycles of Miracles. V. The Assaults on the Miracles—1. The Jewish. 2. The Heathen (Celsus etc.). 3. The Pantheistic (Spinosa etc.). 4. The Sceptical (Hume). 5. The Miracles only relatively miraculous (Schleiermacher). 6. The Rationalistic (Paulus). 7. The Historico-Critical (Woolston, Strauss). VI. The Apologetic Worth of the Miracles. The author then treats the separate Miracles as he does the Parables.

SYNONYMS OF THE NEW TESTAMENT. New Edition, enlarged. 8vo. cloth. 12s.

The study of synonyms in any language is valuable as a discipline for training the mind to close and accurate habits of thought; more especially is this the case in Greek—" a language spoken by a people of the finest and subtlest intellect; who saw distinctions where others saw none; who divided out to different words what others often were content to huddle confusedly under a common term. . . . Where is it so desirable that we should miss nothing, that we should lose no finer intention of the writer, as in those words which are the vehicles of the very mind of God Himself?" This Edition has been carefully revised, and a considerable number of new synonyms added. Appended is an Index to the Synonyms, and an Index to many other words alluded to or explained throughout the work. "He is," the Athenæum *says, " a guide in this department of knowledge to whom his readers may intrust themselves with confidence. His sober judgment and sound sense are barriers against the misleading influence of arbitrary hypotheses."*

ON THE AUTHORIZED VERSION OF THE NEW TESTAMENT. Second Edition. 8vo. 7s.

After some Introductory Remarks, in which the propriety of a revision is briefly discussed, the whole question of the merits of the present version is gone into in detail, in eleven chapters. Appended is a chronological list

Trench—*continued.*

of works bearing on the subject, an Index of the principal Texts considered, an Index of Greek Words, and an Index of other Words referred to throughout the book.

STUDIES IN THE GOSPELS. Third Edition. 8vo. 10s. 6d.

This book is published under the conviction that the assertion often made is untrue,—viz. that the Gospels are in the main plain and easy, and that all the chief difficulties of the New Testament are to be found in the Epistles. These "Studies," sixteen in number, are the fruit of a much larger scheme, and each Study deals with some important episode mentioned in the Gospels, in a critical, philosophical, and practical manner. Many references and quotations are added to the Notes. Among the subjects treated are:—The Temptation; Christ and the Samaritan Woman; The Three Aspirants; The Transfiguration; Zacchæus; The True Vine; The Penitent Malefactor; Christ and the Two Disciples on the way to Emmaus.

COMMENTARY ON THE EPISTLES to the SEVEN CHURCHES IN ASIA. Third Edition, revised. 8vo. 8s. 6d.

The present work consists of an Introduction, being a commentary on Rev. i. 4—20, a detailed examination of each of the Seven Epistles, in all its bearings, and an Excursus on the Historico-Prophetical Interpretation of the Epistles.

THE SERMON ON THE MOUNT. An Exposition drawn from the writings of St. Augustine, with an Essay on his merits as an Interpreter of Holy Scripture. Third Edition, enlarged. 8vo. 10s. 6d.

The first half of the present work consists of a dissertation in eight chapters on "Augustine as an Interpreter of Scripture," the titles of the several chapters being as follow:—I. Augustine's General Views of Scripture and its Interpretation. II. The External Helps for the Interpretation of Scripture possessed by Augustine. III. Augustine's Principles and Canons of Interpretation. IV. Augustine's Allegorical Interpretation of Scripture. V. Illustrations of Augustine's Skill as an Interpreter of Scripture. VI. Augustine on John the Baptist and on St. Stephen. VII. Augustine on the Epistle to the Romans. VIII. Miscellaneous Examples of Augustine's Interpretation of Scripture. The latter half of the work consists of Augustine's Exposition of the Sermon on the Mount, not however a mere series of quotations from Augustine, but a connected account of his sentiments on the various passages of that Sermon, interspersed with criticisms by Archbishop Trench.

SERMONS PREACHED in WESTMINSTER ABBEY. Second Edition. 8vo. 10s. 6d.

These Sermons embrace a wide variety of topics, and are thoroughly

Trench—*continued.*

practical, earnest, and evangelical, and simple in style. The following are a few of the subjects:—"*Tercentenary Celebration of Queen Elizabeth's Accession;*" "*Conviction and Conversion;*" "*The Incredulity of Thomas;*" "*The Angels' Hymn;*" "*Counting the Cost;*" "*The Holy Trinity in Relation to our Prayers;*" "*On the Death of General Havelock;*" "*Christ Weeping over Jerusalem;*" "*Walking with Christ in White.*"

SHIPWRECKS OF FAITH. Three Sermons preached before the University of Cambridge in May, 1867. Fcap. 8vo. 2s. 6d.

These Sermons are especially addressed to young men. The subjects are "Balaam," "Saul," and "Judas Iscariot," These lives are set forth as beacon-lights, " to warn us off from perilous reefs and quicksands, which have been the destruction of many, and which might only too easily be ours." The John Bull *says, " they are, like all he writes, affectionate and earnest discourses."*

SERMONS Preached for the most part in Ireland. 8vo. 10s. 6d.

This volume consists of Thirty-two Sermons, the greater part of which were preached in Ireland; the subjects are as follows:—*Jacob, a Prince with God and with Men*—*Agrippa*—*The Woman that was a Sinner*—*Secret Faults*—*The Seven Worse Spirits*—*Freedom in the Truth*—*Joseph and his Brethren*—*Bearing one another's Burdens*—*Christ's Challenge to the World*—*The Love of Money*—*The Salt of the Earth*—*The Armour of God*—*Light in the Lord*—*The Jailer of Philippi*—*The Thorn in the Flesh*—*Isaiah's Vision*—*Selfishness*—*Abraham interceding for Sodom*—*Vain Thoughts*—*Pontius Pilate*—*The Brazen Serpent*—*The Death and Burial of Moses*—*A Word from the Cross*—*The Church's Worship in the Beauty of Holiness*—*Every Good Gift from Above*—*On the Hearing of Prayer*—*The Kingdom which cometh not with Observation*—*Pressing towards the Mark*—*Saul*—*The Good Shepherd*—*The Valley of Dry Bones*—*All Saints.*

Tudor.—The DECALOGUE VIEWED as the CHRISTIAN'S LAW. With Special Reference to the Questions and Wants of the Times. By the Rev. RICH. TUDOR, B.A. Crown 8vo. 10s. 6d.

The author's aim is to bring out the Christian sense of the Decalogue in its application to existing needs and questions. The work will be found to occupy ground which no other single work has hitherto filled. It is divided into Two Parts, the First Part consisting of three lectures on "Duty," and the Second Part of twelve lectures on the Ten Commandments. The Guardian *says of it, "His volume throughout is an outspoken and sound exposition of Christian morality, based deeply upon true foundations, set forth systematically, and forcibly and plainly expressed*—*as good a specimen of what pulpit lectures ought to be as is often to be found."*

Tulloch.—THE CHRIST OF THE GOSPELS AND THE CHRIST OF MODERN CRITICISM. Lectures on M. RENAN's "Vie de Jésus." By JOHN TULLOCH, D.D., Principal of the College of St. Mary, in the University of St. Andrew's. Extra fcap. 8vo. 4s. 6d.

Vaughan.—Works by CHARLES J. VAUGHAN, D.D., Master of the Temple :—

CHRIST SATISFYING THE INSTINCTS OF HUMANITY. Eight Lectures delivered in the Temple Church. New Edition. Extra fcp. 8vo. 3s. 6d.

The object of these Sermons is to exhibit the spiritual wants of human nature, and to prove that all of them receive full satisfaction in Christ. The various instincts which He is shewn to meet are those of Truth, Reverence, Perfection, Liberty, Courage, Sympathy, Sacrifice, and Unity. "We are convinced that there are congregations, in number unmistakeably increasing, to whom such Essays as these, full of thought and learning, are infinitely more beneficial, for they are more acceptable, than the recognised type of sermons."—John Bull.

MEMORIALS OF HARROW SUNDAYS. A Selection of Sermons preached in Harrow School Chapel. With a View of the Chapel. Fourth Edition. Crown 8vo. 10s. 6d.

"Discussing," says the John Bull, *"those forms of evil and impediments to duty which peculiarly beset the young, Dr. Vaughan has, with singular tact, blended deep thought and analytical investigation of principles with interesting earnestness and eloquent simplicity." The* Nonconformist *says "the volume is a precious one for family reading, and for the hand of the thoughtful boy or young man entering life."*

THE BOOK AND THE LIFE, and other Sermons, preached before the University of Cambridge. New Edition. Fcap. 8vo. 4s. 6d.

These Sermons are all of a thoroughly practical nature, and some of them are especially adapted to those who are in a state of anxious doubt.

TWELVE DISCOURSES on SUBJECTS CONNECTED WITH THE LITURGY and WORSHIP of the CHURCH OF ENGLAND. Fcap. 8vo. 6s.

Four of these discourses were published in 1860, *in a work entitled* Revision of the Liturgy; *four others have appeared in the form of separate sermons, delivered on various occasions, and published at the time by request; and four are new. The Appendix contains two articles,—one on "Subscription and Scruples," the other on the "Rubric and the Burial Service." The* Press *characterises the volume as "eminently wise and temperate."*

Vaughan (Dr. C. J.)—*continued.*

LESSONS OF LIFE AND GODLINESS. A Selection of Sermons preached in the Parish Church of Doncaster. Fourth and Cheaper Edition. Fcap. 8vo. 3s. 6d.

This volume consists of Nineteen Sermons, mostly on subjects connected with the every-day walk and conversation of Christians. They bear such titles as "The Talebearer," "Features of Charity," "The Danger of Relapse," "The Secret Life and the Outward," "Family Prayer," "Zeal without Consistency," "The Gospel an Incentive to Industry in Business," "Use and Abuse of the World." The Spectator *styles them "earnest and human. They are adapted to every class and order in the social system, and will be read with wakeful interest by all who seek to amend whatever may be amiss in their natural disposition or in their acquired habits."*

WORDS FROM THE GOSPELS. A Second Selection of Sermons preached in the Parish Church of Doncaster. Second Edition. Fcap. 8vo. 4s. 6d.

The Nonconformist *characterises these Sermons as "of practical earnestness, of a thoughtfulness that penetrates the common conditions and experiences of life, and brings the truths and examples of Scripture to bear on them with singular force, and of a style that owes its real elegance to the simplicity and directness which have fine culture for their roots."*

LESSONS OF THE CROSS AND PASSION. Six Lectures delivered in Hereford Cathedral during the Week before Easter, 1869. Fcap. 8vo. 2s. 6d.

The titles of the Sermons are:—I. "Too Late" (Matt. xxvi. 45). II. "The Divine Sacrifice and the Human Priesthood." III. "Love not the World." IV. "The Moral Glory of Christ." V. "Christ made perfect through Suffering." VI. "Death the Remedy of Christ's Loneliness." "This little volume," the Nonconformist *says, "exhibits all his best characteristics. Elevated, calm, and clear, the Sermons owe much to their force, and yet they seem literally to owe nothing to it. They are studied, but their grace is the grace of perfect simplicity."*

LIFE'S WORK AND GOD'S DISCIPLINE. Three Sermons. New Edition. Fcap. 8vo. 2s. 6d.

The Three Sermons are on the following subjects:—I. "The Work burned and the Workmen saved." II. "The Individual Hiring." III. "The Remedial Discipline of Disease and Death."

THE WHOLESOME WORDS OF JESUS CHRIST. Four Sermons preached before the University of Cambridge in November 1866. Second Edition. Fcap. 8vo. cloth. 3s. 6d.

Dr. Vaughan uses the word "Wholesome" here in its literal and original sense, the sense in which St. Paul uses it, as meaning healthy,

Vaughan (Dr. C. J.)—*continued.*

sound, conducing to right living; *and in these Sermons he points out and illustrates several of the "wholesome" characteristics of the Gospel, —the Words of Christ.* The John Bull *says this volume is "replete with all the author's well-known vigour of thought and richness of expression."*

FOES OF FAITH. Sermons preached before the University of Cambridge in November 1868. Fcap. 8vo. 3s. 6d.

The "Foes of Faith" preached against in these Four Sermons are:— I. "Unreality." II. "Indolence." III. "Irreverence." IV. "Inconsistency." "They are written," the London Review *says, "with culture and elegance, and exhibit the thoughtful earnestness, piety, and good sense of their author."*

LECTURES ON THE EPISTLE to the PHILIPPIANS. Third and Cheaper Edition. Extra fcap. 8vo. 5s.

Each Lecture is prefaced by a literal translation from the Greek of the paragraph which forms its subject, contains first a minute explanation of the passage on which it is based, and then a practical application of the verse or clause selected as its text.

LECTURES ON THE REVELATION OF ST. JOHN. Third and Cheaper Edition. Two Vols. Extra fcap. 8vo. 9s.

In this Edition of these Lectures, the literal translations of the passages expounded will be found interwoven in the body of the Lectures themselves. In attempting to expound this most-hard-to-understand Book, Dr. Vaughan, while taking from others what assistance he required, has not adhered to any particular school of interpretation, but has endeavoured to shew forth the significance of this Revelation by the help of his strong common sense, critical acumen, scholarship, and reverent spirit. "Dr. Vaughan's Sermons," *the* Spectator *says, "are the most practical discourses on the Apocalypse with which we are acquainted." Prefixed is a Synopsis of the Book of Revelation, and appended is an Index of passages illustrating the language of the Book.*

EPIPHANY, LENT, AND EASTER. A Selection of Expository Sermons. Third Edition. Crown 8vo. 10s. 6d.

The first eighteen of these Sermons were preached during the seasons of 1860, *indicated in the title, and are practical expositions of passages taken from the lessons of the days on which they were delivered. Each Lecture is prefaced with a careful and literal rendering of the original of the passage of which the Lecture is an exposition. The* Nonconformist *says that "in simplicity, dignity, close adherence to the words of Scripture, insight into 'the mind of the Spirit,' and practical thoughtfulness, they are models of that species of pulpit instruction to which they belong."*

THE EPISTLES OF ST. PAUL. For English Readers. PART I., containing the FIRST EPISTLE TO THE THESSALONIANS. Second Edition. 8vo. 1s. 6d.

Vaughan (Dr. C. J.)—*continued.*

It is the object of this work to enable English readers, unacquainted with Greek, to enter with intelligence into the meaning, connection, and phraseology of the writings of the great Apostle.

ST. PAUL'S EPISTLE TO THE ROMANS. The Greek Text, with English Notes. Fourth Edition. Crown 8vo. 7s. 6d.

This volume contains the Greek Text of the Epistle to the Romans as settled by the Rev. B. F. Westcott, D.D., for his complete recension of the Text of the New Testament. Appended to the text are copious critical and exegetical Notes, the result of almost eighteen years' study on the part of the author. The "Index of Words illustrated or explained in the Notes" will be found, in some considerable degree, an Index to the Epistles as a whole. Prefixed to the volume is a discourse on "St. Paul's Conversion and Doctrine," suggested by some recent publications on St. Paul's theological standing. The Guardian *says of the work,—"For educated young men his commentary seems to fill a gap hitherto unfilled. . . . As a whole, Dr. Vaughan appears to us to have given to the world a valuable book of original and careful and earnest thought bestowed on the accomplishment of a work which will be of much service and which is much needed."*

THE CHURCH OF THE FIRST DAYS.
    Series I.   The Church of Jerusalem.   Third Edition.
       " II.   The Church of the Gentiles.   Second Edition.
       " III.   The Church of the World.   Second Edition.
Fcap. 8vo. cloth.   4s. 6d. each.

Where necessary, the Authorized Version has been departed from, and a new literal translation taken as the basis of exposition. All possible topographical and historical light has been brought to bear on the subject; and while thoroughly practical in their aim, these Lectures will be found to afford a fair notion of the history and condition of the Primitive Church. The British Quarterly *says,—"These Sermons are worthy of all praise, and are models of pulpit teaching."*

COUNSELS for YOUNG STUDENTS. Three Sermons preached before the University of Cambridge at the Opening of the Academical Year 1870-71. Fcap. 8vo. 2s. 6d.

The titles of the Three Sermons contained in this volume are:—I. "The Great Decision." II. "The House and the Builder." III. "The Prayer and the Counter-Prayer." They all bear pointedly, earnestly, and sympathisingly upon the conduct and pursuits of young students and young men generally.

NOTES FOR LECTURES ON CONFIRMATION, with suitable Prayers. Eighth Edition. Fcap. 8vo. 1s. 6d.

In preparation for the Confirmation held in Harrow School Chapel, Dr. Vaughan was in the habit of printing week by week, and distributing among the Candidates, somewhat full notes of the Lecture he purposed to

Vaughan (Dr. C. J.)—*continued.*
deliver to them, together with a form of Prayer adapted to the particular subject. He has collected these weekly Notes and Prayers into this little volume, in the hope that it may assist the labours of those who are engaged in preparing Candidates for Confirmation, and who find it difficult to lay their hand upon any one book of suitable instruction.

THE TWO GREAT TEMPTATIONS. The Temptation of Man, and the Temptation of Christ. Lectures delivered in the Temple Church, Lent 1872. Extra fcap. 8vo. 3s. 6d.

Vaughan.—Works by DAVID J. VAUGHAN, M.A., Vicar of St. Martin's, Leicester :—

SERMONS PREACHED IN ST. JOHN'S CHURCH, LEICESTER, during the Years 1855 and 1856. Cr. 8vo. 5s. 6d.

CHRISTIAN EVIDENCES AND THE BIBLE. New Edition, revised and enlarged. Fcap. 8vo. cloth. 5s. 6d.

"*This little volume,*" *the* Spectator *says,* "*is a model of that honest and reverent criticism of the Bible which is not only right, but the duty of English clergymen in such times as these to put forth from the pulpit.*"

Venn.—ON SOME OF THE CHARACTERISTICS OF BELIEF, Scientific and Religious. Being the Hulsean Lectures for 1869. By the Rev. J. VENN, M.A. 8vo. 6s. 6d.

These discourses are intended to illustrate, explain, and work out into some of their consequences, certain characteristics by which the attainment of religious belief is prominently distinguished from the attainment of belief upon most other subjects.

Warington.—THE WEEK OF CREATION ; OR, THE COSMOGONY OF GENESIS CONSIDERED IN ITS RELATION TO MODERN SCIENCE. By GEORGE WARINGTON, Author of "The Historic Character of the Pentateuch Vindicated." Crown 8vo. 4s. 6d.

The greater part of this work is taken up with the teaching of the Cosmogony. Its purpose is also investigated, and a chapter is devoted to the consideration of the passage in which the difficulties occur. "A very able vindication of the Mosaic Cosmogony by a writer who unites the advantages of a critical knowledge of the Hebrew text and of distinguished scientific attainments."—Spectator.

Westcott.—Works by BROOKE FOSS WESTCOTT, D.D., Regius Professor of Divinity in the University of Cambridge ; Canon of Peterborough :—

The London Quarterly, *speaking of Mr. Westcott, says,*—"*To a learning and accuracy which command respect and confidence, he unites what are not always to be found in union with these qualities, the no less valuable faculties of lucid arrangement and graceful and facile expression.*"

Westcott (Dr. B. F.)—*continued.*

AN INTRODUCTION TO THE STUDY OF THE GOSPELS. Fourth Edition. Crown 8vo. 10s. 6d.

The author's chief object in this work has been to shew that there is a true mean between the idea of a formal harmonization of the Gospels and the abandonment of their absolute truth. After an Introduction on the General Effects of the course of Modern Philosophy on the popular views of Christianity, he proceeds to determine in what way the principles therein indicated may be applied to the study of the Gospels. The treatise is divided into eight Chapters:—I. The Preparation for the Gospel. II. The Jewish Doctrine of the Messiah. III. The Origin of the Gospels. IV. The Characteristics of the Gospels. V. The Gospel of St. John. VI. and VII. The Differences in detail and of arrangement in the Synoptic Evangelists. VIII. The Difficulties of the Gospels. The Appendices contain much valuable subsidiary matter.

A GENERAL SURVEY OF THE HISTORY OF THE CANON OF THE NEW TESTAMENT DURING THE FIRST FOUR CENTURIES. Third Edition, revised. Crown 8vo. 10s. 6d.

The object of this treatise is to deal with the New Testament as a whole, and that on purely historical grounds. The separate books of which it is composed are considered not individually, but as claiming to be parts of the apostolic heritage of Christians. The Author has thus endeavoured to connect the history of the New Testament Canon with the growth and consolidation of the Catholic Church, and to point out the relation existing between the amount of evidence for the authenticity of its component parts and the whole mass of Christian literature. "The treatise," says the British Quarterly, *"is a scholarly performance, learned, dispassionate, discriminating, worthy of his subject and of the present state of Christian literature in relation to it."*

THE BIBLE IN THE CHURCH. A Popular Account of the Collection and Reception of the Holy Scriptures in the Christian Churches. New Edition. 18mo. 4s. 6d.

The present volume has been written under the impression that a History of the whole Bible, and not of the New Testament only, would be required, if those unfamiliar with the subject were to be enabled to learn in what manner and with what consent the collection of Holy Scriptures was first made and then enlarged and finally closed by the Church. Though the work is intended to be simple and popular in its method, the author, for this very reason, has aimed at the strictest accuracy.

A GENERAL VIEW OF THE HISTORY OF THE ENGLISH BIBLE. Second Edition. Crown 8vo. 10s. 6d.

In the Introduction the author notices briefly the earliest vernacular versions of the Bible, especially those in Anglo-Saxon. Chapter I. is oc-

Westcott (Dr. B. F.)—*continued.*

cupied with an account of the Manuscript English Bible from the 14th century downwards; and in Chapter II. is narrated, with many interesting personal and other details, the External History of the Printed Bible. In Chapter III. is set forth the Internal History of the English Bible, shewing to what extent the various English Translations were independent, and to what extent the translators were indebted to earlier English and foreign versions. In the Appendices, among other interesting and valuable matter, will be found "Specimens of the Earlier and Later Wycliffite Versions;" "Chronological List of Bibles;" "An Examination of Mr. Froude's History of the English Bible." *The* Pall Mall Gazette *calls the work* "A brief, scholarly, and, to a great extent, an original contribution to theological literature."

THE CHRISTIAN LIFE, MANIFOLD AND ONE. Six Sermons preached in Peterborough Cathedral. Crown 8vo. 2s. 6d.

The Six Sermons contained in this volume are the first preached by the author as a Canon of Peterborough Cathedral. The subjects are:— I. "*Life consecrated by the Ascension.*" II. "*Many Gifts, One Spirit.*" III. "*The Gospel of the Resurrection.*" IV. "*Sufficiency of God.*" V. "*Action the Test of Faith.*" VI. "*Progress from the Confession of God.*" *The* Nonconformist *calls them* "Beautiful discourses, singularly devout and tender."

THE GOSPEL OF THE RESURRECTION. Thoughts on its Relation to Reason and History. Third Edition. Fcap. 8vo. 4s. 6d.

The present Essay is an endeavour to consider some of the elementary truths of Christianity, as a miraculous Revelation, from the side of History and Reason. The author endeavours to shew that a devout belief in the Life of Christ is quite compatible with a broad view of the course of human progress and a frank trust in the laws of our own minds. In the third edition the author has carefully reconsidered the whole argument, and by the help of several kind critics has been enabled to correct some faults and to remove some ambiguities, which had been overlooked before. He has not however made any attempt to alter the general character of the book.

ON THE RELIGIOUS OFFICE OF THE UNIVERSITIES. Crown 8vo. 4s. 6d.

"*There is certainly, no man of our time—no man at least who has obtained the command of the public ear—whose utterances can compare with those of Professor Westcott for largeness of views and comprehensiveness of grasp. . . . . . There is wisdom, and truth, and thought enough, and a harmony and mutual connection running through them all, which makes the collection of more real value than many an ambitious treatise.*"— Literary Churchman.

Wilkins.—THE LIGHT OF THE WORLD. An Essay, by A. S. WILKINS, M.A., Professor of Latin in Owens College, Manchester. Second Edition. Crown 8vo. 3s. 6d.

This is the Hulsean Prize Essay for 1869. The subject proposed by the Trustees was, "The Distinctive Features of Christian as compared with Pagan Ethics." The author has tried to show that the Christian ethics so far transcend the ethics of any or all of the Pagan systems in method, in purity and in power, as to compel us to assume for them an origin, differing in kind from the origin of any purely human system. "It would be difficult to praise too highly the spirit, the burden, the conclusions, or the scholarly finish of this beautiful Essay."—British Quarterly Review.

Wilson.—RELIGIO CHEMICI. With a Vignette beautifully engraved after a Design by Sir NOEL PATON. By GEORGE WILSON, M.D. Crown 8vo. 8s. 6d.

"George Wilson," says the Preface to this volume, "had it in his heart for many years to write a book corresponding to the Religio Medici *of Sir Thomas Browne, with the title* Religio Chemici. *Several of the Essays in this volume were intended to form chapters of it, but the health and leisure necessary to carry out his plans were never attainable, and thus fragments only of the designed work exist. These fragments, however, being in most cases like finished gems waiting to be set, some of them are now given in a collected form to his friends and the public."—"A more fascinating volume," the* Spectator *says, "has seldom fallen into our hands."*

Wilson.—THE BIBLE STUDENT'S GUIDE TO THE MORE CORRECT UNDERSTANDING of the ENGLISH TRANSLATION OF THE OLD TESTAMENT, BY REFERENCE TO THE ORIGINAL HEBREW. By WILLIAM WILSON, D.D., Canon of Winchester. Second Edition, carefully revised. 4to. 25s.

" The author believes that the present work is the nearest approach to a complete Concordance of every word in the original that has yet been made: and as a Concordance, it may be found of great use to the Bible student, while at the same time it serves the important object of furnishing the means of comparing synonymous words, and of eliciting their precise and distinctive meaning. The knowledge of the Hebrew language is not absolutely necessary to the profitable use of the work. The plan of the work is simple: every word occurring in the English Version is arranged alphabetically, and under it is given the Hebrew word or words, with a full explanation of their meaning, of which it is meant to be a translation, and a complete list of the passages where it occurs. Following the general work is a complete Hebrew and English Index, which is, in effect, a Hebrew-English Dictionary.

Worship (The) of God and Fellowship among Men. Sermons on Public Worship. By Professor MAURICE, and others. Fcap. 8vo. 3s. 6d.

This volume consists of Six Sermons preached by various clergymen, and although not addressed specially to any class, were suggested by recent efforts to bring the members of the Working Class to our Churches. The preachers were—Professor Maurice, Rev. T. J. Rowsell, Rev. J. Ll. Davies, Rev. D. J. Vaughan.

Yonge (Charlotte M.)—SCRIPTURE READINGS for SCHOOLS AND FAMILIES. By CHARLOTTE M. YONGE, Author of "The Heir of Redclyffe." Globe 8vo. 1s. 6d. With Comments. 3s. 6d.

SECOND SERIES. From Joshua to Solomon. Extra fcap. 8vo. 1s. 6d. With Comments. 3s. 6d.

THIRD SERIES. The Kings and Prophets. Extra fcap. 8vo., 1s. 6d., with Comments, 3s. 6d.

Actual need has led the author to endeavour to prepare a reading book convenient for study with children, containing the very words of the Bible, with only a few expedient omissions, and arranged in Lessons of such length as by experience she has found to suit with children's ordinary power of accurate attentive interest. The verse form has been retained because of its convenience for children reading in class, and as more resembling their Bibles; but the poetical portions have been given in their lines. Professor Huxley at a meeting of the London School-board, particularly mentioned the Selection made by Miss Yonge, as an example of how selections might be made for School reading. "Her Comments are models of their kind."—Literary Churchman.

In crown 8vo. cloth extra, Illustrated, price 4s. 6d. each Volume; also kept in morocco and calf bindings at moderate prices, and in Ornamental Boxes containing Four Vols., 21s. each.

MACMILLAN'S SUNDAY LIBRARY.

A SERIES OF ORIGINAL WORKS BY EMINENT AUTHORS.

The Guardian *says—"All Christian households owe a debt of gratitude to Mr. Macmillan for that useful 'Sunday Library.'"*

THE FOLLOWING VOLUMES ARE NOW READY:—

The Pupils of St. John the Divine.—By CHARLOTTE M. YONGE, Author of "The Heir of Redclyffe."

The author first gives a full sketch of the life and work of the Apostle himself, drawing the material from all the most trustworthy authorities, sacred and profane: then follow the lives of his immediate disciples, Ignatius,

Quadratus, Polycarp, and others; which are succeeded by the lives of many of their pupils. She then proceeds to sketch from their foundation the history of the many churches planted or superintended by St. John and his pupils, both in the East and West. In the last chapter is given an account of the present aspect of the Churches of St. John,—the Seven Churches of Asia mentioned in Revelations; also those of Athens, of Nîmes, of Lyons, and others in the West. "Young and old will be equally refreshed and taught by these pages, in which nothing is dull, and nothing is far-fetched."—Churchman.

The Hermits.—By CANON KINGSLEY.

The volume contains the lives of some of the most remarkable early Egyptian, Syrian, Persian, and Western hermits. The lives are mostly translations from the original biographies. "It is from first to last a production full of interest, written with a liberal appreciation of what is memorable for good in the lives of the Hermits, and with a wise forbearance towards legends which may be due to the ignorance, and, no doubt, also to the strong faith of the early chroniclers."—London Review.

Seekers after God.—LIVES OF SENECA, EPICTETUS, AND MARCUS AURELIUS. By the Rev. F. W. FARRAR, M.A., F.R.S., Head Master of Marlborough College.

In this volume the author seeks to record the lives, and gives copious samples of the almost Christ-like utterances of, with perhaps the exception of Socrates, "the best and holiest characters presented to us in the records of antiquity." The volume contains portraits of Aurelius, Seneca, and Antoninus Pius. "We can heartily recommend it as healthy in tone, instructive, interesting, mentally and spiritually stimulating and nutritious."—Nonconformist.

England's Antiphon.—By GEORGE MACDONALD.

This volume deals chiefly with the lyric or song-form of English religious poetry, other kinds, however, being not infrequently introduced. The author has sought to trace the course of our religious poetry from the 13th to the 19th centuries, from before Chaucer to Tennyson. He endeavours to accomplish his object by selecting the men who have produced the finest religious poetry, setting forth the circumstances in which they were placed, characterising the men themselves, critically estimating their productions, and giving ample specimens of their best religious lyrics, and quotations from larger poems, illustrating the religious feeling of the poets or their times. "Dr. Macdonald has very successfully endeavoured to bring together in his little book a whole series of the sweet singers of England, and makes them raise, one after the other, their voices in praise of God."—Guardian.

Great Christians of France: ST. LOUIS and CALVIN. By M. GUIZOT.

From among French Catholics, M. Guizot has, in this volume, selected

Louis, King of France in the 13th century, and among Protestants, Calvin the Reformer in the 16th century, "as two earnest and illustrious representatives of the Christian faith and life, as well as of the loftiest thought and purest morality of their country and generation." In setting forth with considerable fulness the lives of these prominent and representative Christian men, M. Guizot necessarily introduces much of the political and religious history of the periods during which they lived. "A very interesting book," says the Guardian.

Christian Singers of Germany. — By CATHERINE WINKWORTH.

In this volume the authoress gives an account of the principal hymn-writers of Germany from the 9th to the 19th century, introducing ample specimens from their best productions. In the translations, while the English is perfectly idiomatic and harmonious, the characteristic differences of the poems have been carefully imitated, and the general style and metre retained. "Miss Winkworth's volume of this series is, according to our view, the choicest production of her pen."—British Quarterly Review.

Apostles of Mediæval Europe.—By the Rev. G. F. MACLEAR, D.D., Head Master of King's College School, London.

In two Introductory Chapters the author notices some of the chief characteristics of the mediæval period itself; gives a graphic sketch of the devastated state of Europe at the beginning of that period, and an interesting account of the religions of the three great groups of vigorous barbarians—the Celts, the Teutons, and the Sclaves—who had, wave after wave, overflowed its surface. He then proceeds to sketch the lives and work of the chief of the courageous men who devoted themselves to the stupendous task of their conversion and civilization, during a period extending from the 5th to the 13th century; such as St. Patrick, St. Columba, St. Columbanus, St. Augustine of Canterbury, St. Boniface, St. Olaf, St. Cyril, Raymond Sull, and others. "Mr. Maclear will have done a great work if his admirable little volume shall help to break up the dense ignorance which is still prevailing among people at large."—Literary Churchman.

Alfred the Great.—By THOMAS HUGHES, Author of "Tom Brown's School Days." Third Edition.

"The time is come when we English can no longer stand by as interested spectators only, but in which every one of our institutions will be sifted with rigour, and will have to shew cause for its existence.... As a help in this search, this life of the typical English King is here offered." Besides other illustrations in the volume, a Map of England is prefixed, shewing its divisions about 1000 A.D., as well as at the present time. "Mr. Hughes has indeed written a good book, bright and readable we need hardly say, and of a very considerable historical value."—Spectator.

Nations Around.—By Miss A. KEARY.

This volume contains many details concerning the social and political life, the religion, the superstitions, the literature, the architecture, the commerce, the industry, of the Nations around Palestine, an acquaintance with which is necessary in order to a clear and full understanding of the history of the Hebrew people. The authoress has brought to her aid all the most recent investigations into the early history of these nations, referring frequently to the fruitful excavations which have brought to light the ruins and hieroglyphic writings of many of their buried cities. "Miss Keary has skilfully availed herself of the opportunity to write a pleasing and instructive book."—Guardian. "A valuable and interesting volume."—Illustrated Times.

St. Anselm.—By the Very Rev. R. W. CHURCH, M.A., Dean of St. Paul's. Second Edition.

In this biography of St. Anselm, while the story of his life as a man, a Christian, a clergyman, and a politician, is told impartially and fully, much light is shed on the ecclesiastical and political history of the time during which he lived, and on the internal economy of the monastic establishments of the period. The author has drawn his materials from contemporary biographers and chroniclers, while at the same time he has consulted the best recent authors who have treated of the man and his time. "It is a sketch by the hand of a master, with every line marked by taste, learning, and real apprehension of the subject."—Pall Mall Gazette.

Francis of Assisi.—By Mrs. OLIPHANT.

The life of this saint, the founder of the Franciscan order, and one of the most remarkable men of his time, illustrates some of the chief characteristics of the religious life of the Middle Ages. Much information is given concerning the missionary labours of the saint and his companions, as well as concerning the religious and monastic life of the time. Many graphic details are introduced from the saint's contemporary biographers, which shew forth the prevalent beliefs of the period; and abundant samples are given of St. Francis's own sayings, as well as a few specimens of his simple tender hymns. "We are grateful to Mrs. Oliphant for a book of much interest and pathetic beauty, a book which none can read without being the better for it."—John Bull.

Pioneers and Founders; or, Recent Workers in the Mission Field. By CHARLOTTE M. YONGE, Author of "The Heir of Redclyffe." With Frontispiece, and Vignette Portrait of BISHOP HEBER.

The missionaries whose biographies are here given, are—John Eliot, the Apostle of the Red Indians; David Brainerd, the Enthusiast; Christian F. Schwartz, the Councillor of Tanjore; Henry Martyn, the Scholar-Missionary; William Carey and Joshua Marshman, the Serampore Missionaries; the Judson Family; the Bishops of Calcutta,—Thomas Middleton, Reginald Heber, Daniel Wilson; Samuel Marsden, the Australian Chaplain and Friend of the Maori; John Williams, the Martyr *of Erromango; Allen Gardener, the Sailor Martyr; Charles Frederick Mackenzie, the Martyr of Zambesi.* "*Likely to be one of the most popular of the 'Sunday Library' volumes.*"—Literary Churchman.

Angelique Arnauld, Abbess of Port Royal. By FRANCES MARTIN. Crown 8vo. 4s. 6d.

This new volume of the 'Sunday Library' contains the life of a very remarkable woman founded on the best authorities. She was a Roman Catholic Abbess who lived more than 200 years ago, whose life contained much struggle and suffering. But if we look beneath the surface, we find that sublime virtues are associated with her errors, there is something admirable in everything she does, and the study of her history leads to a continual enlargement of our own range of thought and sympathy.

THE "BOOK OF PRAISE" HYMNAL,
COMPILED AND ARRANGED BY
LORD SELBORNE.

In the following four forms:—

A. Beautifully printed in Royal 32mo., limp cloth, price 6d.
B.   ,,   ,,   Small 18mo., larger type, cloth limp, 1s.
C. Same edition on fine paper, cloth, 1s. 6d.

Also an edition with Music, selected, harmonized, and composed by JOHN HULLAH, in square 18mo., cloth, 3s. 6d.

The large acceptance which has been given to "The Book of Praise" by all classes of Christian people encourages the Publishers in entertaining the hope that this Hymnal, which is mainly selected from it, may be extensively used in Congregations, and in some degree at least meet the desires of those who seek uniformity in common worship as a means towards that unity which pious souls yearn after, and which our Lord prayed for in behalf of his Church. "The office of a hymn is not to teach controversial Theology, but to give the voice of song to practical religion. No doubt, to do this, it must embody sound doctrine; but it ought to do so, not after the manner of the schools, but with the breadth, freedom, and simplicity of the Fountain-head." On this principle has Sir R. Palmer proceeded in the preparation of this book.

The arrangement adopted is the following:—

PART I. *consists of Hymns arranged according to the subjects of the Creed—*"*God the Creator,*" "*Christ Incarnate,*" "*Christ Crucified,*" "*Christ Risen,*" "*Christ Ascended,*" "*Christ's Kingdom and Judgment,*" *etc.*

PART II. *comprises Hymns arranged according to the subjects of the Lord's Prayer.*

PART III. *Hymns for natural and sacred seasons.*

There are 320 *Hymns in all.*

CAMBRIDGE:—PRINTED BY J. PALMER.

www.ingramcontent.com/pod-product-compliance
Lightning Source LLC
Chambersburg PA
CBHW020908230426
43666CB00008B/1353